HOMEMADE WINE FOR SEASONAL FESTIVALS

Homemade Wine for Seasonal Festivals

HOMEMADE Wine FOR SEASONAL FESTIVALS

Lyn Baylis

Published by Avalonia
www.avaloniabooks.co.uk

Published by Avalonia

BM Avalonia
London
WC1N 3XX
England, UK
www.avaloniabooks.co.uk

HOMEMADE WINE FOR SEASONAL FESTIVALS
Copyright © 2015 Lyn Baylis

First Edition, August 2015
ISBN 978-1-905297-84-9

Original cover art by Chloe Humphries.
Copyright © 2015 All rights reserved.

Design by Satori, for Avalonia.

British Library Cataloguing in Publication Data. A catalogue record for this book is available from the British Library.

All rights reserved. No part of this publication may be reproduced or utilised in any form or by any means, electronic or mechanical, including photocopying, microfilm, recording, or by any information storage and retrieval system, or used in another book, without written permission from the author.

About the Author: Lyn Baylis

A mother of five, Lyn Baylis was born in London in 1949.

Lyn's love of winemaking started at a very early age. Perched on her mother's draining board she would watch her prepare and make wine until finally she was allowed to stir the ingredients and eventually get involved with the whole process. Over the years she shared her winemaking skills with a number of wine-making circles, honing her skill by taking part in competitions.

Lyn is a Multifaith Chaplain to whom spirituality has always been important – it combines with her love of the countryside to give an added dimension to her winemaking. In addition, by paying special attention to the medicinal and spiritual qualities of her ingredients, she began to make wines combining all these elements to create a unique whole.

Lyn grew up in Sussex and has recently retired there, although she has no plans to stop making wines or giving talks on all aspects of winemaking. An advocate of the holistic approach to medicine and natural remedies she is presently engaged in additional research into wine and its curative qualities.

You can write to the author:
    Lyn Baylis
    c/o BM Avalonia
    London, WC1N 3XX
    United Kingdom
        or email - admin@avaloniabooks.co.uk

About the Artist: Chloe Humphries

Chloe Humphries is one of the up and coming young artists of today. She started her journey by studying Art & Design in her home county of Staffordshire, using the ceramics and pottery industry all around her as inspiration. An illustrator at heart, she is happiest using paint, pen and collage in her work but has been known to employ the use of photography on occasions.

She adores handmade pieces and believes that taking time and love to form each piece of individual hand-created work is ever more important with the advancing range of technology at our fingertips.

Find her on www.etsy.com/people/Flojoe89

Homemade Wine for Seasonal Festivals

Table of Contents

PREFACE	9
INTRODUCTION	13
Understanding Wine	18
THE SEASONAL FESTIVALS	22
Making Wine as an Act of Magic	25
The Practicalities of Seasonal Wine Making	27
A Word of Warning	30
Spring Equinox	32
Beltane - May Day	38
Summer Solstice	46
Lammas	51
Autumn Equinox	58
Samhain - Halloween	64
Winter Solstice - Yule	69
Candlemas - Imbolc	73
WINE RECIPES	77
Dandelion Wine	78
Nettle Wine	80
Birch Sap Wine	81
Young Oak Leaf Wine	82
Hawthorn Wine	83
Gorse Wine	84
Rose Petal Wine	85
Elderflower Wine	86

SPARKLING ELDERFLOWER WINE	87
STRAWBERRY WINE	88
BLACKBERRY WINE	89
PLUM WINE	90
MORELLO CHERRY WINE	91
GARDEN CHERRY WINE	92
MEAD - HONEY WINE	93
APPLE WINE	95
ELDERBERRY WINE	96
ROSEHIP WINE	97
SLOE WINE	98
SLOE GIN	99
ROWAN BERRY WINE	100
MIXED BERRY WINE - ENGLISH PORT	101
WASSAIL BOWL	102
WHEAT WHISKEY	103
DRIED FRUIT WINES	104
FROZEN FRUIT WINES	104
TINNED FRUIT WINES	105
FINAL THOUGHTS	107
BASIC REQUIREMENTS FOR COUNTRY WINES	108
GLOSSARY OF TERMS USED	113
PROBLEM PAGE	114
INDEX	**119**

DEDICATION

To Mum and Pa, thank you for sharing your spiritual views and your deep love of nature and for giving me the knowledge and skills to make my own wine, a hobby that has in some ways taken over my life (but in a very good way), and to my children, grandchildren, and extended family for continuing to inspire me.

To Sophie for all her practical help and advice and the kick when I got bogged down, and to Flo (Chloe) for the wonderful illustrations, they finish off the book perfectly. Thank you.

PREFACE

I cannot remember a time when wine making was not an important part of my life. My mother made wines out of just about anything. As soon as I was old enough I was recruited to help with the work of gathering fruit, cutting up vegetables and stirring the must (the initial mixture of fruit, flower or other ingredient plus yeast and sugar) daily. Our larder was full of bottles, buckets and demijohns (fermentation jars), with other demijohns wherever there was an empty surface. One of my earliest recollections is the plop, plop, plop of the fermentation lock in a demijohn on the landing windowsill outside my bedroom. It was almost a lullaby.

I had a very happy childhood. My father, already retired when I was born, looked after me while my mother worked. Each day we took a long walk through woodlands behind our house and over the fields to feed the ponies. During these rambles, he taught me about the spirits of the trees, flowers, animals and birds, and how to feel the energy of all living things, explaining that all life was somehow interconnected. His openness of spirit, and gentle relationship with nature instilled in me a deep love of the wonderful planet on which we live, likewise a desire to understand how I could become more in tune with nature and the spirit world. It has been a lifelong journey, and one that still fills me with awe.

When I was older, I joined a local winemakers group. Thanks to Ernie Turner and Jim Thompson, I became quite proficient as a winemaker and competition winner in my own right - although I must confess my mother's recipes were partly responsible. I've always enjoyed giving talks about wine and wine making, particularly about making wine using seasonal fruit, vegetables and flowers. I have spoken at a variety of venues from our local Church Hall, the WI meeting rooms, a village school for a Parent Teacher Association fundraiser, Fairfield Halls in Croydon and Conway Hall in London. I never cease to feel a thrill when someone comes up to me to say that following my talk they have been inspired to start making their own wine. It is the requests for information on which wines to use for which seasonal festival which prompted me to put pen to paper, resulting in this present work.

I hope you enjoy this book and that it encourages you to make your own wines. It really isn't difficult as long as you have heaps of patience to wait until the wine is ready to be drunk. Believe me, the rewards far outweigh the amount of work involved.

Bottoms up!

Lyn Baylis

Words of Warning

With over 40 years' experience of making wines on my own, I find I am unable to remember the initial source of some of my recipes. Many were my mother's; some are printed here exactly as given to me; some I have altered to suit my taste; others are recipes that have been given to me by friends and colleagues.

Now that I no longer take part in competitions, I don't have to worry about the exact level of alcohol in my wines, although my experience tells me it varies between 12% and 16%.

For those of you not used to country wines, some of the gentle tastes can be deceiving. Believe me, these wines are often much more alcoholic than your average shop bought wine, so please be aware of this!

I take no responsibility for any inebriation which you may experience from drinking wine made using any of these recipes, for any acts which occur as a result of this inebriation or any accidents to the person caused by over imbibing wine made from the recipes in this book.

Right. Now that's the red tape dealt with, let's get on with the fun!

Homemade Wine for Seasonal Festivals

INTRODUCTION

Alcohol of some variety has been used in religious ceremonies as far back as we can trace. The first alcoholic beverage was not wine, but rather beer. Evidence for this rough form of beer has been found in and near Neolithic burials. It is believed that it would have been produced as a by-product linked with the discovery of yeast, possibly during the fermentation of bread.

Initially, it was used primarily in rituals, either as an offering to the Gods or to bring about visions. On the occasions when it was not used in sacred rituals, it is believed to have been a drink that only the very wealthy could afford. However, as mankind became more in control of their lives, their brewing skills also increased.

By 2900 BCE, Sumerian tablets were listing 19 different types of beer and with increased knowledge and skills, this beverage became more and more accessible. By 1913 BCE beer, as we know it, had become an integral part of Egyptian life, with the first public beer house. As well as being the first known place to establish a public beer house, Egypt was also one of the earliest places to mention the use of wine in its rituals.

The Inundation ceremony was an annual ritual which celebrated the inundation or flooding of the Nile, which brought fertility to the land. In 3000 BCE, at this ceremony, the god Osiris was addressed by the title of "Lord of the Wine". It was a commonly held belief that it was Osiris who taught humanity the secret of how to cultivate grapes. Likewise, the god Horus has also been linked to wine - his left eye being represented by white wine, his right by red wine.

Wine was also used to honour Goddesses, evidence for one such example dating to 2000 BCE in which wine was used in the worship of the goddess Pagat in Ugarit. In another recorded example, the Mesopotamian Goddess Ishtar was offered twelve vases of wine daily.

Interestingly however, though wine was used in rituals and ceremonies to worship both Gods and Goddesses, it would appear that Goddesses were linked to wine in a much more direct sense as it was they who controlled the fermentation of the brew and ensured that the wine was good. The Sumerian goddess of the vine is a case in point. If she was unhappy with her people the vines did not prosper, but if she was happy and viewed the offerings of her priests with pleasure, the yield more than doubled.

These practices continued throughout most cultures and by 1500 BCE it can be seen that most brewers had a favoured Goddess whom they invoked to ensure that their wine was of the best quality. One of those so invoked was the snake goddess Renen-utet, as shown by the numerous small shrines and figures representing her, which have frequently been found near the wine presses.

Wine soon became the favored drink for the wealthy and for sacred rites throughout the civilised world, A wide variety of types has been found amongst the grave goods of the pharaohs. Wines made from barley, dates, and pomegranates became popular around the time of Ramses III (1187 to 1156 BCE). Roman wines were still made with grapes and flavoured with herbs and flowers. However, regardless of this, wine does not appear to have been made available to the ordinary man, possibly because it was viewed as sacred until around 1000 BCE. Even then, the populace did not wish to give up their beer!

In Greece, Dionysus was credited with introducing the vine and causing the rivers to flow with wine rather than water, and there is evidence that both he and Poseidon were offered wine as part of their rituals. Anthesteria, one of the four Athenian festivals in honour of Dionysus, was held every year over a period of three days, around the time of the February full Moon. This festival appears to have been celebrated by both the Athenian and Ionian cities (Ionia is present day Turkey).

The festival of Anthesteria and the others that took place around this time celebrated the successful fermentation and the excellent quality of the newly matured wine. Great emphasis was given not only to the bounty of the land, the wonderful taste of the grapes, and the subsequent delicious brew - but the festivities also brought about a relaxation in the normal state of affairs. The usual privileges of status and position during this time were allowed to slip. In many instances, the accepted family systems were overturned to allow connections that could not be sanctioned at any other time of the year. For example, slaves were sometimes included in festivities which would normally have been exclusively for the family unit.

Family ties, of course, were imperative - and it appears that at this very special time, efforts were made to reconnect with all members of the family, bringing everyone together. It was an opportunity for integrating new friends into the family, introducing them to relatives often resulting in the development of new and useful political and cultural alliances, which continued long after the festivities finished.

In the Roman Empire, the God of wine, Liber, was not as popular as Bacchus, and by 200 BCE Bacchus, the Greek deity, was being worshipped in Rome. The Roman Senate were happy with this situation believing that if a much-loved god such as Bacchus was watching over the soldiers they would be able to preserve the city from the Carthaginians and others. This worked for a time, but the popularity of Bacchus, which had started out as an asset, now became a threat, with the emergence of the many and varied cults of Bacchus. With more and more ceremonies devoted to the god, the Senate began to fear the development of new conspiracies fuelled by the rites and rituals of the spreading Bacchanalian cults. They worried that these well-liked cults would undermine their fundamental aims and duties and, turning against Bacchus, they finally moved to suppress the upsurge of Bacchus worship in 186 BCE, culminating in the suppression of the female cult of the Bacchanalia. As the Romans advanced through Britain and Gaul in the Second Century CE, they brought with them their taste for wine and, following their invasion of Britain, wine became the accepted drink.

Wine has always been used in ritual and in religious ceremonies and is still a crucial part of many religious gatherings today. In the UK, the most widely known ceremony using wine would be the Catholic mass or any other Christian Communion Service. However, when it is used in services other than those of the Roman Catholic Church, the wine only symbolizes the blood of Christ. The Catholic Church teaches that the wine, when blessed by the priest during the celebration of Mass, goes through a process called transubstantiation, which is when it becomes, not symbolically, but in actuality, the blood of Christ.

Wine is often mentioned in the Bible, and it is evident that it was available and, although probably not a widespread drink, was kept for special occasions. The story of Christ changing the water into wine at a wedding feast is one of the best known Bible stories, and is also referenced at the Last Supper, the final meal when Christ and his disciples gathered together, drinking wine with their dinner.

In nature-based or Earth-centred religions in the UK, the image of a knife plunging into a chalice of wine is a familiar symbol, which represents the union of male and female. It is often used in modern fertility rituals or in more complicated ceremonies, when it represents the joining of the God and Goddess in a sacred act, one which brings blessings on all who partake of the wine, sharing in the bounty of the land and the fertility of the Gods

It can be seen that wine still has a very particular status, even in our modern society when the amounts of cheap wine make it available to everyone. Although it may often be thrown down the throat on a drunken night out, there are still times, those particular times, when it is sipped with reverence and savoured as part of a much bigger occasion.

Understanding Wine

'*Wine*', from the Latin *Vinum*, is generally accepted as being the fermented juice of the grape. However, country wines can be made from any suitable fruit, vegetable, grain or leaf with the addition of sugar and yeast, plus an occasional extra ingredient. The natural fermentation process works as the yeast turns the sugar into ethyl alcohol and carbon dioxide.

For many centuries, wine was brewed in kitchens using earthenware bowls and jugs covered with cloth. The yeast used initially was almost certainly baker's yeast. It was spread on bread or toast and floated on top of the brew. This process was a little hit-and-miss and often allowed a good wine to be ruined by a bacterial infection. In particular, potato wine could, in less than careful circumstances, produce an amount of methyl alcohol as well as the required ethyl alcohol. This caused heavy drunkenness, excessive headaches and hangovers and, very occasionally when taken in large quantities, was known to cause blindness.

However, we have progressed a long way from the times gone by. Cleaniness and carefulness are still key considerations, but we can make good and well-balanced country wines for any occasion without spending a lot of money on ingredients, by gathering fruit etc., from the hedgerows and fields, or by growing our own produce.

On the subject of cleanliness and carefulness, I used to take part in quite a few local wine competitions and festivals but, with a young family, finding the time to bottle the wine and get exactly the right presentation often proved difficult. On one particular occasion, having had a very busy day, I finally managed to get my husband his dinner and put the children to bed before quickly cleaning the kitchen area I needed to work in. I did a quick taste test and chose the best of my wines, bottled it and labelled it correctly etc., and rushed off to the festival. I usually did quite well at these events so imagine my surprise to find that my wine had a card next to it reading "Booby Prize." I was even more amazed when it was announced that I had made the best OXO wine that the judges had ever tasted!

To this day, I don't know how it happened. I am so particular about keeping my preparation area clean and sterilising all the items I need to use. I can only think that a grain of the OXO stock cube I had used when making my husband's dinner had clung to my dress and somehow when I was bottling the wine it had fallen into the open bottle.

A cautionary note: when gathering from the hedgerows, ensure that it is not alongside a busy road, as the fruit and flowers will have been contaminated by exhaust fumes. Also, do check first that the fields where you gather from have not been sprayed with chemicals.

Here are a few poisonous ingredients to steer clear of. This is NOT an exhaustive list, so the basic rule of thumb is that if you are in any doubt about an ingredient, **DO NOT USE IT.**

Poisonous Ingredients – Do Not Use!

Acacia

Aconite

Anemones

Aquilegia

Arum Lilies

Azaleas

Baneberry or any plant that has bane in its title (this means poison)

Bay tree leaves

Berberis

Black nightshade

Bluebell

Buckthorns (Alder and common)

Broom

Buttercup

Campion

Celandine

Columbine

Charlock

Clematis

Cotoneaster

Crocus

Cyclamen

Daffodil

Dahlia

Deadly nightshade

Delphinium

Dwarf elder

Ferns

Fool's parsley

Foxglove

All fungi

Geranium

Green potatoes

Groundsel (ragwort, fleawort etc.)

Any of the hellebores

Hemlock

Henbane

Holly

Honeysuckle berries

Horse chestnut

Iris

Ivies

Laburnum

Laurel

Lilac

Lily of the Valley

Lobelia

Lupine

Marsh Orchid

Meadow Rue

Meadow Saffron

Mercury (annual and dog)

Pheasant's eye

Peony

Poppies (various)

Privets (garden hedge, oval-leaved, British native)

Rhododendron

Rhubarb (except stalks)

Soapwort

Spindle tree

Pea (broad-leaved everlasting, sweet pea)

Thornapple

Tomato (except for fruit)

Traveler's Joy

Tulips

Wood anemone

Woody nightshade

Yew

The Seasonal Festivals

In the British Isles, when country people lived in harmony with the land, their lives were bounded by the hedges of the village fields, their primary pathways the country lanes between these. What we now know as seasonal festivals sprang from their early celebrations to mark the changing seasons.

Over the passage of time, these festivals became formalised, with people coming together to celebrate, commemorate, or just to forget the harshness of their lives for a while, enjoying themselves at a particular time of year. (Sometimes, the place they gathered was also crucial.) The two natural rural calendars which emerged were the *agricultural* and the *pastoral* calendar.

The *pastoral*, the earlier of the two, was slowly overpowered by the later *agricultural* cycle and largely lost its identity. However, on close scrutiny, we can deduce that Candlemas, or Imbolc, was the lambing festival. May Day or Beltane, marked the date when the new grazing was expected to be ready. Lammas, or Lughnasadh, appears to have been the date when the shearing finished and fairs were held to exchange stock, while Hallowmas or Samhain saw the rounding up to the flocks and herds, the slaughter of surplus animals and the mating of the sheep. In addition, the Pre-Christian British festivals, particularly those celebrated around December and January were (by the instructions of the Pope) to be closely associated with the church's festival days, and, in complying, it happened that the original pastoral festival days became completely absorbed into the Christian calendar of festivals.

The agricultural calendar was sufficiently close to the Solar Solstices and Equinoxes for them also to be incorporated into the festival year. The still extant quarter days, which marked the agricultural year are Lady Day (25th March), Midsummer Day (24th June), Michaelmas (29th September) and Christmas (25th December).

As modern society evolved, these eight celebrations became an integral part of a yearly pattern, The ensuing wheel of the year brought together two systems to form one complete structure which is now accepted by many as being the way to reconnect with the natural cycle and energies of the Earth. The eight festivals that are now celebrated are Imbolc/Candlemas, Spring Equinox, Beltane/May Day, Summer Solstice, Lammas, Vernal Equinox, Samhain/Halloween and Yule/Winter Solstice.

I have given suggestions of the wines which can be made at each seasonal festival. This list is based on the fruit, flower, or other ingredients that are usually ripe and available at this time. However, as nature by her very essence is unpredictable, you will discover that this list is not always accurate, but I trust that it is useful to as a guideline, and, as I said with the oak wine, if it is not ready at the precise moment you want to make the wine, you end up watching it, and in that process, you learn a lot about the tree or whatever it is you are waiting for.

Over the last few years, because of the increasingly hot summers, blackberries, which are typically seen in late August, have been found in July, and strawberries have been found to fruit in May. If this trend continues, we may have to rethink when we make our wines.

Making Wine as an Act of Magic

Making wines for use as in the Seasonal Festivals is as much a part of any ritual as would be the making of incense, for example. It is a magical act, and, like every other act of magic, your state of mind, your intentions, and your mood are a contributing factor.

Before you set out to gather the ingredients while you are gathering, and for the duration of the whole wine making process, the intent with which you brew your wine is paramount. This intent may have no particular significance other than the hope that all who will drink it will be made whole and happy. Where I grew up, there was a saying *wine made in sour frame retains the sourness*, and, over the years, I have found this to be true. So even though the weather is just right, the plants/trees are just right - unless you are just right, don't even think about making wine.

When we make wine, we work not just on a physical level, but also on a spiritual level. Every tree, plant, leaf, and flower is a part of the same life force that flows within ourselves, and each one has a higher self, as do we.

Organisations like Findhorn have been working with these nature spirits for years. They call them Dryads, and this is the name that I will use although they have been known by many names over the years, including angels, and the hooded ones, a name given them by a number of older country people.

When you are first starting out to make wine, you will find that the easiest spirits to sense are the tree Dryads. Most people standing near to a tree can feel the energy field that radiates from it. If at first you cannot feel this energy, then stand or lean against the tree, close your eyes and imagine yourself being absorbed by the tree and allow yourself to become one with it. If you do this a few times, you will begin to feel the subtle energy of the dryad, and once they have become apparent, you will wonder how you ever failed to notice them.

When you approach a tree to pick its fruit, its flowers or its leaves, always approach it with respect and an open heart. Remember, it is important that you have thought through the purpose of the wine you wish to make before you approach the tree. You don't have to speak out loud, unless, of course, you want to, but it is useful if you can explain what qualities in particular you require. Then wait for a minute to allow the Dryad to withdraw its life force, leaving just sufficient to give you the qualities you need, before you pick the fruit or take the required part.

It is more difficult to feel plant energy, but even if you cannot feel the plant energy at first, act in the same way as if you were approaching a tree, and transmit your thoughts, feelings, and requirements before you pick the leaves or flowers. Do not get despondent if you can't immediately feel plant energy; it may take many visits before you can.

The Practicalities of Seasonal Wine Making

I make my wines mostly from natural ingredients and cannot sufficiently stress how important it is to gather the ingredients when they are at their best. Flowers should be picked when fully opened but before they begin to droop; and they should be dry, so remember to wait until the dew has evaporated.

The ideal time to gather blooms is when the Sun is as near its peak as possible, so that the flower is open, saturated with the Sun's energy and consequently at its most potent. Avoid petals or leaves which have been attacked by insects or are diseased and be very careful not to remove all the flowers/leaves from one plant. If you are following a recipe which requires you to take the whole plant, check first that it is not a protected species, and even should this not be the case, ensure that there are plenty more of the same plants left in the area. In addition, be very careful where you are gathering; make sure plants have not been sprayed with artificial spray. These agricultural sprays are man-made chemicals, and if you continuously use ingredients which have been sprayed, their effects are accumulative and cannot be voided from the human body in the way that natural products can. Another point to remember is that although plants on the sides of main roads may look bonnie, they will have gathered an accumulation of traffic waste, so it is best to leave them well alone and go in search of others less contaminated.

While I must admit that finding, gathering and preparing the ingredients for festival wines can be very time-consuming, if approached with the correct attitude of mind, it can become a seminal part of each festival's preparation. Allow yourself the luxury of unhurried time in which to totally immerse yourself in the gathering experience. Feel the presence and power of the time and place, as well as the form and colour of the season. Immerse yourself in the "now." Then, and only then, should you start searching for whichever plant, flower, leaf, or another ingredient you have decided most optimizes the current festival.

Consider carefully the gathering process. This will depend on your individual beliefs or feeling, but in any case, it can be a time for you to be alone with your thoughts or your deities, or to strengthen the family unit by sharing this experience, or enjoying a natural environment, relaxing in the company of a group of like-minded friends. However you plan the outing, it will help you realize the uniqueness of each season and make you more aware of the essence of that particular time of year, as well as the reasons behind any imminent festival. Not only that, you will also find it to be very therapeutic.

If possible, start the wine on the same day you gather the ingredients. If you can make the gathering and commencement of the winemaking part of your seasonal festival, it will give a more holistic feel to the whole celebration. If you are unable to do this, make sure that you store each ingredient separately and in a way which will not damage them i.e. not crushed, wet, etc.

Why not give over a whole day to the seasonal festival? Our ancestors knew better than we do how important our links with the land are. They never rushed their festivals and although with the pressures of modern living we can no longer extend these celebrations over a week, or for even three or four days, I see no reason why we should not dedicate just one day when we can relax and give ourselves over to the celebration of the seasons, possibly involving all the family in the early preparations or just getting the children to stir the must. If you are lucky, they too, in the same way I did, will get hooked on the whole process.

The wine you start at this year's festival will be ready for next year's celebration and if this seems too long to wait, my own practice is to make two gallons, one which can be drunk after approximately 6 months, and one for next year's festival. If it is not possible for you to make two gallons, then place three bottles aside for next year's ritual use and sample the remainder after the requisite 6 months - with, of course, the excuse that you have to ensure that this year's stock will be worth waiting for until next year!

Don't forget to make a note of the ingredients used. When you started your wine, when you racked it and when you bottled it. It is a useful tool when looking back at your year to know which ones you want to make again. Sometimes you may need to amend the recipe, if, for example, you couldn't collect enough flowers, but need to make the wine that day, you can add for example a small tin of wine concentrate, or 1lb of raisins to the brew. If you write it in your book, you may well find that you have stumbled upon a better taste. As you get more experienced your notebook will help you understand why you like some wines and not others which ones work for you and which ones do not, and in time you will be able to add your own recipes.

I mentioned earlier that the old women of our village used to say *wine made in sour frame retains the sourness*. I'm sure there was a second part to this, but I can't remember what it was; perhaps someone out there can jog my memory. The nearest I can come to it is *wine made in joy will be a joy to drink*. Therefore, with good reason, I wish you joy in your celebrations and in the preparation of your wine.

A Word of Warning

Do investigate the laws regarding the brewing and consumption of wine and alcohol in your own district and country before making your own.

In the UK, there is no restriction on the amount of wine you may make, providing that it is solely for domestic use, that is, used by yourself, your friends, and your family.

You must not sell any of it, for not only will you be breaking the law, but you may find yourself the subject of a customs and excise investigation. Although it seems a little draconian, believe it or not, this prohibition is also extended to occasions such as cheese and wine evenings, as I found out to my horror when we tried to raise funds for my children's school. It was pointed out to me (fortunately before we had started the evening and in time to dash to the shops for replacements) that if we charged for the evening event we could be said to be selling the wine. Likewise, the knowledgeable parent - who was also a police officer - further advised me that we could not put any of the bottles into the raffle as the same rules would apply.

It is possible to sell small amounts of wine if the wine is marked and used solely for religious purposes, but as was explained to me, this opens you up to being investigated in the same way as any other catering operation, and you would need to comply with health and safety regulations. The minimum requirement, I am told, would be a separate sterile area where the wine is made and two sinks. However customs and excise are very vigilant so if your small amounts of wine became more than that, they would investigate you.

On the subject of the UK law around homemade wines, it is illegal to separate out the alcohol by freezing or by any other means. Distillation by any method is not only illegal, but dangerous. The alcohols that are produced this way cannot be said to be safe, and there are hefty penalties if you are caught trying to do this.

Spring Equinox

*In March and April from morning to night
In sowing and setting, good huswives delight
To have in a garden or other like plot
To trim up their houses and to furnish their pot.*

- Thomas Tusser

Spring Equinox is the time when day and night are equal. In many traditions, this is a transitional phase when the Holly guardian of the forest hands over the mantle of guardianship to the Oak, who is gaining in strength and energy. It is also a physical and spiritual transitional phase when people take the time to balance their energies and take the thoughts and ideas generated at the time of Imbolc (Candlemas) to start putting them into practice. Spring clean your house, your garden or your sacred space. Look at it with new eyes and new insights gained during the winter months.

Recollections

When I was a child, St George's day was quite a celebration on two fronts. My mother would start her wine making for the year, and us children would go out, armed with buckets, to pick dandelion heads from the fields. This always took a long time as we got side tracked making daisy chains and picking buttercups to see who liked butter. However, we always remembered to be home by 4 o'clock with well-washed hands (we did not want to wet the bed that night, a commonly held belief that this is what happened if you picked dandelions and did not wash your hands) for a special tea made by my mum for the little band of gatherers which was composed of myself, the Williams girls and the Berry boys. Homemade scones were hot from the oven, with real butter and the mums' special strawberry jam. We all felt exceptionally important. On the Saturday nearest to St George's day, we children all took part in a fancy dress competition in the field just outside the village. I remember the three legged races (mainly because I wasn't very good at this!), coconut shies and all sorts of stalls selling jams, cakes and, of course, mum's scones, which always sold well. There would be some variety of band playing, the adults dancing and singing, while we children ate a lot and played various games and probably made nuisances of ourselves until we were finally taken home to bed, tired, sleepy.

Now

The winter has been very mild, and all the trees are budding. I go to check on the oak, but find that the leaves are not yet ready for picking. Across the road, there is also an ash, and this looks much more advanced. Remembering the country rhyme, I hope it isn't going to prove correct.

> *Oak before Ash we're in for a splash*
> *Ash before Oak we're in for a soak.*
>
> *- Traditional*

Over the last few years, I have found that the oak is coming into leaf a little later than it used to, and I have mostly picked the soft new oak leaves at Beltane.

Older and wiser, I am now aware of the equinox and all it means, it is a time of equal day and night, light and dark, good and bad. A time of balance, when we should all allow ourselves the time to take a long hard look at our busy lives. Is this what we want for the next year, are we truly happy the way we are? Are we putting into practice the ideas and plans made at Imbolc?

Now is the time to be honest with ourselves, remembering to trust our instincts and our intuition, as well as listening to the logical, rational side of our brain. Those are doubly blessed who can achieve a state of balance both inside and out, physically and mentally, for when we treat our bodies with respect and love and listen to the ancient inner wisdom that is deep within each one of us, we can achieve balance within ourselves, and having achieved this balance, we can deal with the practicalities of modern living, using the balanced energies flow to work through our physical, mental and spiritual selves to keep us healthy and attract other balanced energies into our lives.

What is it about these plants?

Dandelion

In March, there are a number of flowers in evidence: the primrose, the wood anemone, and the celandine to mention just a few, but none of these are appropriate for making wine. The first wine I make each year is dandelion wine. The traditional day for picking the dandelions and making this wine is April 25th - St George's Day or Shakespeare's birthday.

Dandelions have long been used for kidney and liver disorders, and it is its use as a diuretic which has brought about its bad reputation, which, instead of us using the grand name of *Taraxacum Officinale*, caused country people to call it piss-the-bed and other similar names. It is combined with other ingredients for use to clear skin diseases and also dyspepsia.

Dandelion is a very Mercurial weed associated with the element of air. It opens us up and develops our psychic abilities, allowing positive energy to heal and purify while defeating any negative energies that remain.

It has long been linked to the underworld and is known to be beloved by bees. In folklore, bees often act as a psychopomp (the guide who/which takes a living soul to the place of the dead, or alternatively the figure who walks in our dreams), which is why dandelion, as well as allowing creative and illuminating dreams, is often taken by those who walk between realms and commune with the spirits who reside in both places.

OAK

The English Oak can come into leaf as early as the end of March (which, of course, is ideal), or as late as the end of May. So although Spring Equinox would be the best time to make the wine, it is not always possible to do so. Over the past few years, I have found that the earliest time that I can make oak leaf wine is Beltane, therefore I have included the recipe for oak leaf wine and information on oak as part of the Beltane wine making. You may find that this year the oak leaves are out at the solstice, and just by watching the tree's progress, you will have already started your immersion in nature's cycle, and have experienced the pleasure of the hunt. Make the wine at the appropriate time, when the tree and leaves are at their best, and store for next year celebration.

NETTLE

Don't forget the Common Nettle. It is often treated as a weed and removed by gardeners, but it has been used for centuries as a food being rich in vitamins A & C, as well as sodium and iron. It is an exceedingly good pick-me-up and a nutritious spring tonic, cleansing the body of toxins and unnecessary carbohydrates gathered during the winter months. Used to give strength and help pregnant and lactating women with their milk production, Hippocrates recorded 61 medicinal uses of the plant in the fourth and fifth centuries BCE.

Stinging nettle is well known as a means to drive out negativity and unwanted spirits and is mentioned in the nine herbs charm(an Old English Charm from the 10th Century).It is a male plant, being associated with the Celtic Sun God, the element of fire and the sign of Scorpio because of its fiery nature.

Nettle energises and sets free any spirit trapped in winter's lethargy and enables us to break away from any negative energies, whether they are self-imposed or sent by others. It provides the momentum which lifts us physically, mentally and spiritually, seeing the way forward with knowledge and clarity and helps earthbound spirits to fly again.

(Note: During the last war nettles were recognised for their nutritional value and Dr RA Butcher, the National Herb Organiser, set up Country Herbs Committees, who gathered the nettles. It was noted that in 1942, ninety tons of dried nettle were collected.)

BELTANE - MAY DAY

Oh we've been rambling all this night
And sometime of this day
And now returning home again
We bring you in the May.

We bring you in the May my friends
We bring you in the May
And wish you love and wish you luck
And wish you joy this day.

- Traditional

Beltane was originally a celebration of the Celtic God of Light, Belenus or Bel, the shining solar hero; this was a time when Bel fires were lit to encourage and strengthen the Sun into life-giving warmth. The hilltops blazed with twin fires through which the cattle were driven to ensure their health and fertility.

Later, the May Day celebrations continued with Maypoles set high on the hills. These were either Pine or Hawthorn and were brought into the village at Sunrise to the accompaniment of loudly blown horns and flutes. Later in the day, people would dance the maypole.

To our ancestors, these festivals were for ensuring fecundity of humans, as well as crops and beasts.

Old Beltane took place over 8 days from the 1st to the 8th of May. This was a magical time. An old Scottish saying runs "You have the skill of man and beast if you were born between the Beltanes."

Perhaps these 8 days explain why the Helston Floral Day with its "Flurry dancers" is held, not on May Day, but on May 8th each year.

Older still is the Jack in the Green, a man completely dressed in green and covered with greenery dancing under a weighty frame. He is the representative of Spring itself and all over Europe there are counterparts, such as Green George and the Wild Man from the Swiss forests to name just two. In the country, the Green Man is known to walk the earth, waking nature from her winter sleep. His passage brings lush green growth to the land and fertility to man and animals alike.

RECOLLECTIONS

A few years ago, I spent what was, to me, the perfect Beltane. We rose early and climbed our local hill to watch the Sun at dawn come up over the horizon. Then, running home (yes, even me!), I cooked up one massive (calorie loaded) breakfast. A couple of hours "rest" and we were ready to venture forth again, first to pick the may blossom to make our first batch of hawthorn wine, then on to our local public house, there to sit "in right good company" on a grassy bank, leaning against a large oak tree, on that oh-so-Sunny day with a glass of cider in hand. The icing on the cake was our local Morris team, much laughter, fun, good dancing and their boisterous, happy music. Eventually we made our way to our site, to commence our own private Beltane festivities. The last act before retiring to bed? Stirring the mush of hawthorn blossom.

NOW

May Day morning and I climbed out of bed to officiate at a dawn handfasting (traditional marriage ceremony). It was a simple, yet beautiful ceremony, the woodland glade bisected by a small scurrying stream. The couple so in love, I felt honoured to be part of their lives, their happiness infectious. The early birdsong and rising Sun added to my sense of contentment.

I allowed myself a few minutes to feel at one with the natural world, before thanking the spirits of the place for their great gift. Life had been so busy up to that point; as well as the usual day to day duties, I had been practicing maypole dancing with the children from the school who were still worried about dancing in a public festival over the weekend. They needn't have worried; they were brilliant.

Again, this year, no blossom on the Hawthorn and, for me, Beltane doesn't truly start until the May (Hawthorn) is in blossom.

At last, and seemingly overnight, it happened! One day it wasn't there and the next day the branches were weighed down with Hawthorn blossom. Had I somehow missed a couple of days? Life had got busy and complicated. Regardless, the hawthorn is out, and today is dry, the sky is bright clear and blue. Today we start the preparations; tomorrow we gather the blossoms and start off the wine. Then we can truly start our own May celebrations.

What is it about these plants/trees?

YOUNG OAK LEAF

It seems appropriate if you are just starting to make festival wines to start with oak leaf wine. The oak, after all, is about to accept the mantle worn by the Holly all winter and to take up his responsibilities as guardian of the summer forest.

The English oaks can come into leaf as early as mid-March (which, of course, is ideal) or as late as the end of May. Should this not be the case this year, then make the wine at the appropriate time: i.e. when the tree and leaves are at their best, and store for next year.

The oak is an ancient symbol of strength and courage in so many British stories and myths. It was used for all types of construction, but mainly houses, churches, boats and ships because of its strength and durability. Therefore, oak leaf wine can be taken when there is a need for these qualities. Oak is also known in Welsh as Darwen, with similar words in both Scottish and Irish meaning door. Drinking the young oak leaf wine can open the door to new beginnings and bring inner peace to anyone suffering from spiritual and mental problems, giving the protection of the guardian of the forest to them as they struggle to find firmer ground.

Cowslip

Folks tell me that the May's in flower
The cowslips-peeps are fit to pull
And I've leave to spend an hour
To get this little basket full.

- Traditional

The Cowslip peeps (flowers) were made into wine by my mother, but recently the plant seems to have gone into a decline, and the Cowslip has become a protected plant. If you would still like to make this wine, it is possible to buy the seeds and you can grow a small patch for wine making purposes, so please do not go out picking wild plants. Cowslips are mentioned in many herbals as renowned for healing headaches, convulsions, and nerve pain while ointments made with the flowers were sprinkled on ladies faces as a remedy to drive away wrinkles and freckles. It is another golden and Sunny plant which has been linked to Venus, the Roman Goddess of love and fertility, and also has connections with the Norse Goddess Freya. A small amount of cowslip blossom (cultivated) in spring water will cleanse the face. Wash your face with spring water, with or without the cowslip peeps, and drink a little of the wine. You will find all sorts of possibilities surround you, provided you open your heart and let love in.

Hawthorn

> *Here we come gathering nuts and May*
> *Nuts and May, nuts and May*
> *Here we come gathering nuts and May*
> *On a cold and frosty morning*
>
> — Traditional

Of course it is impossible to gather nuts at the same time as May blossom, but my understanding is that nuts is a corruption of the word knotts, that is, knotts of flowers, which were traditionally gathered on May Day by the children.

Hawthorn, or the May Tree, is acknowledged by many as the Mother tree. Hawthorn (mother), Oak (father) and Ash (the Everlasting Child) were traditionally tied together with red thread as a protection against evil.

> *Oak Staff, strength and security*
> *Ash wand of immortality*
> *Blossoming bough that bears the May*
> *Three together bound today*
>
> *Oak the father, Hawthorn Mother,*
> *Ash the child of ancient spring*
> *'Gainst harm from earth, sky, sea, or fire*
> *Magic three, protection brings.*
>
> — Anonymous

Its links with the love and the heart are numerous, with tea made from berries, leaves and the May blossom stimulating the circulation and it is also an aid for many types of heart condition. I usually make Hawthorn blossom wine to drink at this festival. It has a nutty and yet very clean taste. It opens the heart to the wonders of love, which is very apt at this fertility festival, and in addition it brings relief from anxiety and stress. Sometimes it is difficult to collect sufficient blossoms of this plant, as the flowers do not last long. It is therefore often necessary to gather the blossoms at a time when you are unable to complete the wine making process. If this occurs, place the flowers in brown paper bags and suspend to allow them to dry out, or lay them out on a surface or tray until you can utilise them.

Silver Birch

The silver birch appears very fragile but is an amazingly resilient tree. It is one of the first to regenerate after any sort of natural disaster, so it is known as the survivor tree. It reminds us that even where there appears to be weakness, there is the potential for incredible strength, and stands as an inspiration and a symbol of the resolve and persistence of those starting out on the path in their lives or in their spiritual development.

As it regenerates, it leaves space and air within the woodland which allows smaller plants to grow safe within its care, and so teaches us that we should not stifle those we care for - but give love, guidance, and the ability to find their own way.

Wine from this tree will bring about purification and renewal. It has associations with Venus and is connected to both the elements of air and water. It is a good wine if you are trying to cut away from old habits or negative energies and it helps the formation of new beginnings. Wine made from the silver birch is wonderfully thick and rich and is made from the sap. A hole is drilled 2 inches deep at 45 angle into the trunk and a tube is inserted to collect the sap; you will need to plug around the tube to prevent spillage, and to preserve the tree, you should only take one pint then plug the hole.

Gorse

> *"It raises the spirits and washes away the dark thoughts of winter."*

The golden-yellow gorse is a pioneer which colonises disturbed ground scenting the air with its strong heady perfume. It is often planted where there are very young trees to act as protection and shelter. The golden flowers of the gorse reflect the growing strength of the Sun. It is associated with the Celtic Sun God and gives protection against the darkness of winter and evil spirits.

If you feel that life or you are stuck in a negative place, then gorse will lift you, balancing your energies to ease frustrations and bring a feeling of deep inner joy. Where there is depression, it gives hope; where there is a weakness, it brings strength; where there is hopelessness it brings hope and self-belief. It is a plant that promotes new and creative thoughts that give illumination to the soul and renewal to the body. Within its shelter, we can take the time to restore our faith in ourselves. Like all golden flowers, it has connections with the element of fire and is said to attract money.

Gorse flowers open at the start of spring and bushes have been found in blossom practically all the year round, which gave rise to the old country saying 'When Gorse is out of bloom, Kissing's out of season' and the custom of inserting a spray of Gorse in the bridal bouquet is an allusion to this, which is why it is commonly known to inspire love.

My father used to talk about the smell of the gorse in Moose Valley, Canada, a place he stayed at when a young man. Indeed, he told me he could close his eyes, smell it, and be immediately transported back to that time and place and feel just for a short time that he was again that young man, sitting in the sunshine taking in the beauty of the valley, and being totally content. I know that these visions sustained him in the last few months of his life when he was bed bound. So for personal reasons, as well as the acknowledged properties of the gorse, when I can, you will find me drinking this wonderful tasting wine and filling myself with the colours and the cheerfulness of the spring sunlight, anticipating new and fresh ideas.

SUMMER SOLSTICE

With solstice Sun high in the sky
The veil between the worlds is thin
Then natural and unknown may merge
Tho' summer's fires light the green.

- Anonymous

Summer Solstice is the longest day of the year. The Sun is at the height of its power, but also there is recognition that this is also the time when the Sun's power will start to dwindle and the knowledge that, from now onwards, the days will be getting shorter. In common with most of Northern Europe, the British Isles continued to light bonfires on hilltops for Midsummer Night until well into the 18th Century.

Midsummer is a time of fertility and fullness, the pregnant earth, healthy and glowing. The world is in balance and yet it is one of those "in between" times. Fire and passion at night, fire and passion during the day…

The night, Female time, the day the time of the Male, combined at this magical time. Not the frantic urgent coupling of Beltane, but a mature, leisurely, gentle and thoughtful coupling, bringing completion to a loving union. Its symbolism is the red rose used with elderflowers to decorate the sacred groves where couples would gather to ask for fertility. This is thought to be the motivation behind the custom which called for couples wishing for a baby to make love at high noon, preferably at sacred sites on Midsummer Day to produce a strong, healthy and beautiful child.

Recollections

I can't remember the exact date, but it was about a month before school broke up for the summer holidays, so probably around the summer solstice, and it always seemed to be a hot day. (In photos I'm usually wearing a bonnet. I hated wearing hats but suffered from sunstroke, so was made to wear one.) There was a Summer Fair, with lots of penned in animals to see and feed, displays of all kinds, the local ballet group, the cubs and scouts, brownie and guides all had a spot, followed by displays of horsemanship culminating in a Medieval Jousting match, and for those who didn't ride, there were good-natured wrestling matches. Well... mainly good natured, although I dare say a few grudges were ironed out at this time. Looking back, it was the young men strutting their stuff most of the time. I suppose it was appropriate with the Sun, the most glorious male symbol at its peak!

Everyone was there. It was a community day and we went to the club in the evening for a barn dance, shared food all laid out on a trestle table at the end of the hall. Outside, the non-dancers gathered around a huge bonfire and sampled homebrew and other delights.

Now

Lying in the grass, I think back to those carefree days of childhood as I gaze out across the fields, through purple clover, white daisy, golden buttercup and a screen of green grasses. An insect walks up the blade of grass beside me, such a small creature, yet perfect in its own way. I feel warm and alive, basking in the afternoon Sun. This is an extraordinary place and comforted by the peace and tranquillity, I remember what really matters to me. Time passes; it only seems a minute, but a fresh breeze blows making the grasses dance. It feels good, but it is a gentle reminder that time is passing and I must begin to make my way home.

I rise and dance a few steps barefooted, enjoying the warmth of the Sun on my head and shoulders. I wonder what my neighbours would make of me! On Midsummer Day, I will dance beneath the Sun, I will stir my rose petal wine. And in the evening, I will dance beneath the Moon, by the midsummer fire. Then I will sit and commune with friends and unseen folk, before losing myself in my own Midsummer Night's Dream.

What is it about these plants/trees?

Elderflower

> *Elder is The Lady's tree*
> *touch it not*
> *or cursed ye be*
>
> - Traditional

Elder has always been related to the Hag or the Goddess, its full blossom has a clean taste and makes an incredible wine and sparkling champagne. These days we can't use the term champagne for wines not made in the Champagne district, but this was the name I grew up with. I guess we now have to call it Sparking Elderflower wine, but it doesn't have the same feel to me. Sparkling Elderflower wine was always made and kept for those special occasions when, if we had been a little better off, we would have opened a bottle of champagne. We use both the dark berries and the white blossoms of this tree and in doing so, it reminds us of the continuing cycle of life or birth and of death.

At this season of the year, it challenges us to look at closely at our life and to accept whatever we discover. This means acknowledging our achievements and recognizing our errors. As the cycle is a continuous motion, we cannot go back but we can venture forward with a surer understanding of ourselves. Its gifts to us are those sweet dreams which illuminate the mind by bringing clarity and ease to emotional turmoil and nagging worries.

Sparkling Elderflower wine and strawberries on a beautiful summer's day will certainly set the scene for those couples who want to conceive a child. As we've already mentioned, couples who were having difficulty conceiving would go to sacred hills and sacred groves to make love at midday; now they are more likely to be found at Cerne Abbas or the Long Man, or on any hill. With the Sun at its height and as high (and as near the God) as possible they lay upon the earth, the bosom of the Goddess, so that the powers of both deities may combine and enable them to conceive.

Strawberries

Blessings from the Gods

With their high iron content, strawberries are excellent for people suffering from anaemia. They are also rich in salicylic acids to aid kidneys, liver and joints. Linne, a famous botanist, referred to them as "blessings from the Gods," having cured his gout by eating almost nothing but large amounts of strawberries morning and evening. In addition, they lower blood pressure and ease gastro problems. Externally, they are used as a beauty treatment and an aid to those seeking love,

This fruit is purported to be the favourite of the Norse Goddess, Freya.

Rose petals

The wild rose, or dog rose, has five petals and was said to be sacred to Venus and Aphrodite.

The large dusky red roses have always been associated with passion and sexuality and mature love while the white rose was the rose of the virgin and symbolised purity. All roses are said to be sacred to Freya, containing within them both elements of fire and water.

White rose petals are incredible for inducing a feeling of peace and harmony, while dark red or scarlet (preferably made using highly scented roses), when taken by lovers, is said to lead to romance and bring a lasting and contented relationship. The fragrant smell, however, hints at exotic pleasures and is said, when used by those within a committed relationship, to ignite spent passion. Doubtless this would also work for those, not in a committed relationship.

Because of their wonderful smells, they were carried in posies by the wealthy to mask the street odours. They were scattered in the path of brides into the church or wedding venue bound into the bride's bouquet and thrown upon both the bride and groom as they emerged as a married couple.

Lammas

Harvest home and the sky is clear
Crying the neck, boys full of cheer
Guisers cavort around the hall
Maid sits with master. All is well

—   Traditional

Lammas appears to have been a particularly Anglo-Saxon occasion. The name Lammas is derived from the Anglo-Saxon "Hlafmaesse" or loaf mass, a festival in which loaves of bread were consecrated. These were made from the first ripe corn.

Here in Britain, the 1st of August usually finds most farmers with much of the harvest still to complete. But then the expectation of a good harvest is also a cause for celebration, and the completion of the first cut a grand excuse for a gathering.

The first cuts were decorated and ceremoniously offered up to the spirit who had dwelt within the seeds throughout the growing season. Often, one sheaf of corn would be set alight as a suitable offering. This was followed by dancing, and 'measured' swigging of the cider, apple wine or beer. (After all, the men would have to resume work early the next morning!)

The other popular name for this time of year is Lughnasadh. This Celtic celebration was to honour Lugh, the God of Light.

Recollections

The Sun is high in the sky and the fields are turning golden brown. In the distance, I can hear the rumble of the machines as they slice through the shimmering carpets. The days have been too hot to walk far, so I have waited for the coolness of night. Beneath the Moon, I walk the paths between the corn, listening to its whispers in the night breeze. Once, it seems a lifetime ago -but the memory is still so strong -, a young man and I walked the corn paths and lay on an old blanket beneath the Moon. We honoured the Lord and Lady and watched the dawn break over the nodding swaths. There was no sacrifice, but an awareness that we would be going our own separate ways from that day and would possibly never meet again. Then, hand in hand we walked back down the hill to the village, breathing in the welcoming smell of freshly baked bread.

This was one festival when we did not make the seasonal wine as part of the festival day. Living in a rural area, all hands, even the children, were roped in to help while the men brought in the harvest; there was no time to go out gathering and making wine.

Now

Now, of course, things have changed, I no longer live on a farm, but I often look at the golden grain and watch the massive combine harvesters ploughing their way through the swathes of corn. It is still a relief when the first cut is made and the skies are still blue. I can imagine how our ancestors felt, praying for the good weather to last. Sadly, there do not seem to be as many poppies, and where they are, they seem to be in small groupings or around the edges of the fields. Modern farming has its advantages and its disadvantages.

Lammas and the Sun are shining. By nine o'clock in the morning, it is already scorching and I sit in the garden relishing the feel of the Sun on my skin. The doorbell sounds and I hear my name called as my friends come in. They bring freshly baked bread with butter and chunks of cheese. I get out the apple juice, the last two bottles saved for this day. We will soon be making some more, as well as the apple wine and cider.

What is it about these plants/trees?

Apple

"An apple a day keeps the doctor away"

Apple has always been a sacred and magical tree. Eating this fruit is reputed to give a knowledge of good and evil and protection from unseen dangers. Its white or pink flowers blossom in the May time and the heavily laden boughs in the summer speak to us of abundance. Cut horizontally, the apple reveals the five pointed star.

Its lesson is that that we, too, should open our hearts to the abundance in our lives, to give freely and with love, knowing that we will be looked after. It reminds us to be grateful for all we have. Once the heart is open, the spirit of the apple tree will open our minds and the positive life forces will allow good things to come to us. As well as carrying all the natural benefits of the apple this wine will also help to heal the wounds of the heart.

Both fruit and juice have tremendous health benefits because of the range of vitamins, minerals, nutrients, and organic compounds that are found in them. The fruit is used as a tonic and cleanser and aids constipation while fruit and juices are quoted by many medical revues as being a defense against tumours and cancer. (Researchers from the University of Oxford found that eating an apple every day could be just as effective as statins in preventing vascular deaths among people over 50.)

Cider was traditionally drunk by the harvesters at this time of year. (It has all the qualities of apple juice.)

Plum or Damson

This fruit comes in a magnificent panorama of colours. Our European plum is thought to have been discovered around two thousand years ago, originating in the area near the Caspian Sea. Even in ancient Roman times, there were already over 300 varieties of European plums.

The fresh version (plums) and the dried version (prunes) contain *phenols* (antioxidants) and help with stomach problems and constipation. They are also a superb source of vitamin C, which promotes a strong immune system and increases the absorption of iron into the body.

It is revered from China and Japan and all the way across Europe, symbolising youthfulness and vitality. Its five petals, like those of the dog rose, are sacred to Venus and Aphrodite, and are often linked to those wonderful creative artists and their delicate paintings and scripts. The plum is said to enhance the qualities of endurance, patience and persistence.

For those challenged by doubt, lack of energy or trapped in darkness, plum provides a strong and loving energy which is healing and very supportive. It will lighten the mind, heart and spirit, giving ease to the heart sore and a youthful vitality, inspiration, determination and resolve.

CHERRY

The cherry is a very low-calorie fruit packed full of nutrients, vitamins, minerals and antioxidants. Antioxidant compounds which are found in the slightly sour or tart cherries are said to inhibit cancer, aging and neurological diseases and can help with the conditions which cause diabetes.

It is visible in much Japanese art, the flowers are fragile and beautiful, the tree strong. It is associated with Venus, containing both water and earth elements.

The earth element in cherry brings with it a very substantial and grounded energy, which gives us the ability not only to see the way through obstacles, but the strength to overcome them. This ability is also used for clairvoyance, divination and medium work while the water element working on the emotions can bring healing and love or fertility. Tales tell, however, that when used to excess, the elements which invoke love can instead provoke envy or desire and lust.

Mead or Honey Wine

The bee has for thousands of years been considered sacred and honey, the bee's gift, hailed for its healing and antibacterial properties. A thin coat of honey can be applied directly onto the skin to disinfect and heal minor skin wounds and chapped lips. It also helps indigestion and has sometimes been used to treat cardiovascular disease and respiratory complaints, as it enhances physical stamina and improves our immune systems.

Taliesin wrote his "Song of Mead" around AD 550, a story of warriors boasting in their halls while feasting and drinking mead and this saga is also repeated in the epic poem Beowulf. Always accepted as a magical brew, the secrets of mead making were kept in the old abbeys and monasteries. Although Lindisfarne is no longer a monastery, the mead that is produced there is known across the world for its wondrous properties.

Drinking honey wine has a calming effect on the mind and promotes sleep (itself a healing agent); the awakening person may find that they have much more energy than before. It is also good for all diseases of the mind, body and spirit, bringing the imbiber a new awareness of themselves and a clearer insight. Where spiritual growth has been stunted by the requirements of the physical world, mead will bring enlightenment and the ability to see beyond the mundane, clearing away the dark areas of the spirit to bring healing and renewed growth.

Rum Pots

Start to make a rum pot to use up all the leftover fruit. It's very easy to do. As indicated by the name, rum was the original spirit used, but brandy, gin or vodka will do equally as well.

An equal quantity of fruit, sugar and chosen spirit is put into the rum pot and occasionally stirred. Save it until Yule or Candlemas for an excellent and very potent reminder of summer.

Autumn Equinox

*Seasons of mists and mellow fruitfulness,
Close bosom-friend of the maturing Sun;
Conspiring with him how to load and bless
With fruit the vines that round the thatch-eves run.*

- John Keats

Autumn Equinox is a time of balance when day and night are equal. It is a transitional phase when the oak, who has been guarding the forest throughout the summer, hands over the mantle of guardianship to the holly, who will stand strong and true throughout the winter, giving shelter to some and food to many more small animals and birds. From now on, the night gains in ascendance.

It is the end of the harvest period of crops, vegetables and fruits and time to celebrate nature's abundance. We have always celebrated what can only be called Harvest Festival at this time of year. Red wines at this time remind us of the God who laid down his life willingly at Lammas and of the blood of all of those who have also laid down their lives so that we may have the freedom to live our lives as we please.

Recollections

I have always loved the autumn. As a young child, some of my earliest memories are of my father sweeping up the leaves in our garden and me throwing myself into each massive mound he created. He never seemed to mind the disruption to his work and laughed with me as I emerged covered in leaves from the bottom of the pile. Sometimes he would pick me up and fling me in the air before throwing me back into the middle of the biggest pile of leaves. What should have been an hour's work could take all afternoon, but I'm sure he didn't mind.

Our Harvest Festival was held in September. I remember that we talked about the Harvest Moon so I assume it was on or near the Sunday of the Harvest Moon. That is the full Moon that occurs closest to the autumn equinox (around 23rd September) This was a religious occasion but in the village there was only The Upper Room which was tiny and with no dedicated priest or vicar most events took place in the hall. Every year we children would go out with baskets and bags to collect blackberries, apples, hawthorn berries and any other fruit or flowers we could find in the hedgerow so that our parents could decorate the hall. John would bring in bales of straw for us to sit on, and some were cast about to make the hall look like a barn. At tea time we would go home and get dressed up while Mum sorted out bottles of wine to take , and baked three loaves of bread,(looking back it would be easy to say the number was very significant, but to be honest it was that number for very practical reasons Mum only had three bread tins). We would then check through the larder for any produce we had spare or tins of food that had been there for a while. Everything was placed in a basket and off we went to the harvest festival. These baskets were later shared among the families in the village and surrounding area who did not have much in the way of produce or money.

I can't really remember much about the service other than we always sang 'All Things Bright and Beautiful' which was one of my favourite hymns. Everyone brought food to share and there was a friendly rivalry, I later learned, to use autumn fruit or vegetables in as many dishes as possible. So there was always lots of food, and mum was not the only winemaker so there was always plenty of wine for the grownups. I drank homemade ginger beer, and occasionally was allowed a shandy,

When the vicar left, Reg would start the entertainment singing all the old songs with Charles accompanying him on his accordion. Sometimes others would do their party pieces, There was something warm and comforting sitting there snuggled up between my parents singing songs we all knew, doing hand movements to some and trying not to get them wrong! Such a happy occasion and so much laughter. I was eventually carried home a sleepy but happy child.

Now

Autumn and the weather is so changeable, dry and bright one day, dark and gloomy the next. Then comes the rain, fierce, and forceful, dashing again and again against the side of our house trying to gain entry. I curl up safe and secure inside, but it serves as a sharp reminder that the balance is changing, the seasons are in flux and winter is on its way. In the copse behind my house the oak leaves are changing their colour; it will not be long before they start falling. Yet beside the oak, the holly stands green and crisp, ready to accept the mantle worn by the oak all summer. Once again at the Equinox, the time of balance, He will take on his responsibilities as guardian of the winter forest.

I arise to a bright morning, and a blue sky. This is the kind of day that calls to you, "come out of your house, bask in my warmth, I cannot promise it for long", so out I venture. The hedgerows are full of wild fruits. This year there are fewer blackberries and sloes, but an abundance of crab apple, elderberry, rowan, and damsons. For me, this is the right harvest festival, and I gather a basket full of these fruits to decorate my house for the evening's celebrations.

What is it about these plants/trees?

Elder

Elder is the Lady's tree, touch it not or cursed ye be.
- Traditional saying

There are many claims as to the healing and health giving properties of the elder, but these may all be as the result of the proven enhancement to the individual's immune system brought about by these berries. Elderberries are known to improve vision on the mortal plane, but they also open the soul to visions on the spiritual plane

The elder is known by country people to be protected by the mother, which is why they will never cut or use elder without first asking the mother and advising why the flower, berry or wood is required. At this time of year, its dark berries, which give prophetic visions, are used to link us with the Crone, who guards the cauldron of renewal and regeneration.

As the nights get darker, we retire into the home, into the womb, being the cauldron of knowledge. In the darkness, we rest in safety, and it is a place where we can look at those things we need to address and seek knowledge of ourselves, accepting the truth and looking for the divinity within. Its healing properties dealing with confusing or emotional turmoil allow the recipient to move on. If we take the time to meditate and review our dreams and our lives, learning and growing in spirit, traveling astral style while we wait in the dark time, we can await springtime knowing that it brings renewal. Therefore, work for inner growth, prosperity and protection or any type of transformation work

BLACKBERRY

Farmer rejoyce at the blackberry winter
Frosted dew on blossoms so early in spring
Will set all the berries and grant us rich harvest
What seems a misfortune, true blessings will bring.

- Anonymous

The Blackberry is among those plants with the highest fibre content in the world, which helps the digestive system. It is high in Vitamin C which gives protection to the immune system, as well as lowering the risk of certain types of cancer. The dark berries produce an antioxidant which reduces inflammation and promotes healthy skin.

The "vine" of the Druidic tree alphabet is said by many scholars to refer to the blackberry or bramble, and in some regions it was considered dangerous to partake of the berries in any form as they belonged not to man but to the faerie realm. Used in worship to the pagan deities of Europe, and also linked with Venus, it was said to bring joyful intoxication which freed the spirit, causing impulsive and often unbridled behavior of a sexual or passionate nature. It can, however, bring new enthusiasms which, if channelled correctly, are transformative, opening the mind to innovative ideas and the inspiration to make them into a reality. The deep, dark juice will also give protection through the winter months from all types of malevolent energies.

Blackberry pie is baked at this festival as part of the autumn harvest celebration bringing happiness and joy to body, mind and spirit.

Rosehip

This is the fruit of a rose. The rose used mostly because of its large and abundant hips is the wild dog rose. These hips are picked once the white fragrant dog rose has bloomed, and all the petals have fallen off.

Rose hips have a high vitamin C and vitamin A content, which help to regenerate skin cells, giving the skin more elasticity to aid better healing of both wounds and scars. They also contain antioxidants which prevent cardiovascular disease and are said to be a cancer preventative.

Rose hips are associated with love and the planet Venus, They carry with them all magical properties of the rose, bringing love, healing and peace.(See rose petals-Summer Solstice.)

Samhain - Halloween

And two long glasses brimmed with muscatel
Bubble upon the table.
A ghost may come

— All Souls Night, W.B. Yeats

Samhain was the second most important fire festival in the Celtic world, the first being Beltane. Many have forgotten this reality, and they no longer link the bonfires of November with this ancient festival. The burning of the Guy was a later addition, and when the fires died down, the young couples would begin leaping through them; in some areas, flaming barrels of tar were rolled from the top of a hill.

There are a number of reasons our ancestors celebrated the festival of Samhain: to give thanks to the Gods for the safe gathering in of the season's crop; to allowed the people to cull the weak animals and lay them down for winter; to note the passing of the Old Celtic year and the start of the new. At this time, it was believed that the God had entered into the underworld, and for a while, the veil between the worlds was thin, allowing the deceased to return. The night was a time of darkness and fires burnt in houses everywhere to keep any evil spirits away. These fires spread into the hills and wheels of straw covered in tar were carried in procession, which were later burnt, on fires everywhere, to herald in the New Year.

Recollections

As a child, Halloween seemed to be one big party. The seeds had been prepared for the spring, and the adults had dealt with the other farmyard chores. We were allowed to help with the preparation of cakes and biscuits and other party foods for the feast: the Halloween party.

It was a grand occasion. Some dressed up in costumes that reflected earlier years while others brought out musical instruments and sang songs. We children gathered around the record player and thought we were the best, learning to jive with the older children.

I don't think I noticed that the company was split earlier in the evening, which it must have been, but later as the candles were lit and we had played all our records, I do remember that we rebels joined our parents taking part in many fun games such as apple bobbing, before listening to Peter, who could play different characters with a change of voice, enthralling us with tales of knightly deeds and derring-do, before finally being sat around the fire happily singing folk songs, songs from musicals and other favourite songs that we all seemed to know. A few days later and it was Bonfire night; dressed in coats, hats and scarves we went around with torches and gathered the local children to come and watch the lighting of the bonfire. Then followed fireworks, racing around the wood with sparklers (not something that would be allowed now!), finishing up with soup and sausages. Amid much laughter and disappointed tears, we children were put to bed while the adults sampled Mum's homemade wine.

Now

The weather has been quite kind to us this year and, when possible, I have taken the time to walk down into the forest. I never cease to be enthralled by the Sun glinting through the trees onto the carpet of red, gold and russet. Even the air carries the hint of winter, with the heady smell of damp earth laced with the scent of bonfires. I cut out a pumpkin, place a candle inside and leave it outside my door. The village children know that this is the sign that I welcome the trick and treaters. The little ones come with their parents, usually two or three families together, the older ones later in the evening. I keep the sweets and fruit in my cauldron and love watching their faces as they try to decide which they should choose. At 10 o'clock I remove the pumpkin and we start our own festivities.

This time when the veil between the worlds is thin, my own family gather together to honour the ancestors and possibly to make contact with loved ones who have gone before, Many people have been raised to fear this time, but in reality it is a time to seek the truth through the darkness and practice divination which may allow us to understand the inner mysteries, so that through acknowledgement and understanding of the unknown we can prepare for the hard times to come.

What is it about these plants/trees?

Rowan Berry or Mountain Ash Berry

The rowan has always been a magical tree. With its orange-red berries, it is linked to the element of fire and to the Sun. It is known for its protective qualities, and although many associates it with Imbolc, it is equally as powerful and appropriate to this dark time of year when people feel low mentally or physically, have dark thoughts or fears or suffer undefined. The rowan with its colourful berries and ability to survive where no other tree could give us its strong message that we must ever hold strongly to our beliefs and never give up on them. It strengthens and balances our energies, giving us protection from the all unwanted manipulations and influences.

At this time of year, its vivacious and vital life force, more than any other, will help to increase our psychic abilities, as well as our ability to communicate with the spirit realms, which in turn will allow us to receive visions and insights to what??

The Rowan has very high vitamin C content, but as the seeds contain traces of prussic acid, it is necessary to boil the berries before use. A common treatment for scurvy and a gargle for sore throats, its astringent properties are also supposed to be good for piles.

Sloe or Blackthorn Berry

Of all the trees that grow so fair,
Old England to adorn,
Greater are none beneath the Sun
Than Oak and Ash and Thorn.

- Rudyard Kipling

The blackthorn berry or sloe is rich in vitamin C and, therefore, useful for all circulation problems. Its fruits, sloes, are dried and used to treat kidney, stomach, and bladder disorders.

Blackthorn can also be used for protection from any malevolent spirit and physical or mental illness that surfaces in the dark time of year. In fairy tales such as *Sleeping Beauty*, it is the blackthorn which hides and protects the magic castle from intruders and princes alike. So we must be aware that the threats to us may come from beyond us, but they may be caused by our own negative attitudes and our inability to recognize these.

In order for us to emerge from the thicket, we must face up to the darker elements within ourselves and be confident that we do not continually hide behind that which protects us. We can then, fortified and renewed, enter the light walking eagerly forward, with the knowledge of who we are, what we want and be ready to deal with for whatever life throws at us.

Winter Solstice - Yule

*Come bring with a noise,
My merry, merry boys,
The Christmas log to the firing
While my good dame she
Bids ye all be free
and drink to your heart's desiring*

- Herrick

Winter Solstice, or Yule, is the end of the cycle of darkness and the beginning of the time of light which begins with the birth of the Sun God. Yule is celebrated on the 21st December, although the original celebrations are reputed to have ended on the 25th December when the priests would have been able to see that the light was returning.

Our ancestors believed that unless they performed their fire rituals and lit many bonfires, the Sun would not return. Families or communities burnt the Yule Log; this was usually oak (considered to be a sacred tree), although in areas of Devon and Cornwall it was reputed to have been an apple log. The Yule Log, once lit, was allowed to burn itself out. The remaining stump was carefully collected, and according to various sources, either kept in the household - to prevent fires throughout the coming year or buried in the ground.

Recollections

As Christmas time draws nearer, the whole neighbourhood seemed to be involved in a frenzy of baking. Christmas cakes cooked earlier in the year were iced, the pastry was rolled to make mince pies and sausage rolls and other party fare, but the main event was the stirring of the pudding.

Every member of the family took turns to stir it and secretly make a wish. Each year my mum would "find" the silver coin, ring and thimble, which were duly stirred into the mixture. These we had been told would bring particular gifts to the finder. The ring promised a wedding, the thimble a life of single blessedness, the coin good fortune. On Christmas Day, a sprig of the holly with the brightest red berries would be stuck in the top of the pudding and then heated, brandy lit and poured over it in a river of fire.

Now

Over the years I have found that by celebrating the Winter Solstice, with all the trimmings of Christmas and the extra ceremony of lighting the Yule Log and calling on the Sun to return, my entire family are able to attend. They can then spend Christmas with their own families or loved ones while I can relax by my open fire and generally eat, drink and do what I like. I am able to enjoy the peace and quiet, whilst watching everyone else still rushing around. I usually give small bunches of ivy, holly and pine tied with red ribbon to all my friends and those whom I wish well during the New Year. These are to protect them from ill during the coming year and were initially given as a protection against Witchcraft!. If they are still fresh on 12th Night, they predict a year of good fortune. I also give them, providing I have enough, a small bottle of mead with which to salute the turning of the year and the return of the Sun.

As the evening draws in, we light many candles to call in the Sun. This is the time to bring our dreams into the light.

Mixed berry wine

We have discussed the elder, the blackberry and the sloe; the only other fruit within this wine is the blackcurrant.

Blackcurrant

The Blackcurrant is known by many because of the liqueur Crème de Cassis, a sweet, dark red brew prepared from blackcurrants. Cassis liqueur was first produced in the 16th century by French monks, at which time it was as a cure for "snakebite and wretchedness."It was also considered to be one of the angelic fragrances and was imbibed by those embarking on a spiritual quest. It is one of the fruits used to open the inner eye as an aid for healing or for clairvoyance.

Wheat Whisky

Wheat is linked with the element of earth and can be traced back to the Neolithic age when it was first cultivated. With women being the first cultivators of the land, it is hardly surprising that all the ancient religions had female harvest deities, many of whom had wheat sheaths within their symbols.

In ancient Greece, wheat and sweetmeats were thrown at newly married couples. In Rome, bride and groom wore wreaths of wheat and lilies which symbolize their purity and fertility. In Egypt, wheat is among the grave goods found in the pharaohs' tombs. In Norse mythology, wheat is sacred to Frey and a symbol of prosperity and protection.

Candlemas - Imbolc

The Snowdrop in purest white arraie
First rears her head on Candelmas daie
While Crocus hastens to the shrine
Of primrose love on St Valentine.

- Taken from an old verse which gives a calendar of flowers for the year

Candlemas, or Imbolc, is the time when we become aware of the very first signs of spring. The snowdrop; a delicate looking flower which somehow manages to force its way through the hard and frozen earth to greet the Sun.

The birth of lambs across the country is showing that new life is returning to the land. (the Celtic words Imbolc (*Oimelg* or *Im Olk*) generally translated as ewes milk, or in the belly). Either way this was very much a pastoral fertility festival linked with Bridie or Bride, who became known as St Bridget, the patron saint of shepherds. Celebrated on the 2nd February it has strong links with Candlemas and the purification of the Virgin Mary, whose candlelit processions can be traced back to the 7th Century.

However, our ancestors saw this as a time of renewal and purification long before this. A time to celebrate the passing of winter, the arrival of Spring and the reawakening earth. In Scotland and Wales the tradition of placing a doll which represented Brede, often in a bed of straw in the fireplace overnight with a wand to represent the male is still reputed to continue. The purpose: to ask for regeneration, and fertility of crops, animals and humans.

In Hereford, the blessing of women coincided with the first digging of the fields. At dusk on the eve of Imbolc candles were lit to drive away the last vestiges of darkness and of winter, and in the morning a bowl of snowdrops was carried into the house, by the youngest member of the household if possible, to purify it and all "in-dwellers from the ravages of winter".

Recollections

I have happy childhood memories of a winter's night spent at my friend's farm. One of the ewes was experiencing a particularly awkward birth. Her father has been gone for a long time, and we children had come down claiming we couldn't sleep and were allowed to stay curled up on the couch near the stove. Our persistence was rewarded, the ewe and lamb pulled through and we were the first to see the tiny new life. My friend's father collapsed into his chair by the Raeburn with a hot toddy and we, too, were given hot toddies before being bundled off to bed. (Although, in retrospect, ours were probably only warm blackcurrant juice!) To me, this is Imbolc. New life to the land, new life to all of Nature's creatures and a promise of better things to come.

It is a celebration of the reawakening earth, new lambs, and the first flowers. At this time of year, there are possibly only snowdrops peering through the ice and snow, but these exquisitely fragile flowers are a visible promise of what is to come.

Now

At this time of year, we can take time out to prepare ourselves for the year ahead and the changes that will occur as the season progresses. Candles are lit at this time to strengthen the power of the Sun and to reinforce the warming of the land. In our climate, there are no plants from which to harvest a seasonal wine, therefore, for me, a hot mulled wine made, if possible, from a mixture of summer fruits, brings an echo of summers gone and remind us that summer will come again, giving us hope and a promise for the forthcoming year. It reminds me that even when the weather seems at its coldest, the warmer days will come. With spring just around the corner, it is a chance for me personally to renew my connections with the earth and the wonders of nature.

With all of nature waiting for the spring and no fresh fruits, leaves or vegetables with which to make wine, it is a good time to take stock of the wines made during the previous year and to decide which are your favourites and which are not quite what you would have liked. Be honest with yourself. Is it a matter of preference? Would you prefer the wine dryer or sweeter? The problems that can occur to home wine brewing do not occur that often, but if something is not quite right see the 'Problem Page' section later in this book.

There may be some that you were unable to make because of weather conditions at the time (Don't lose heart. Even experienced wine makers lose the occasional gallon, but it is generally only the odd one.)

This is the time to venture into your local brewer's shop to buy dried fruit and make the wines you are lacking. I'm not saying that it will be the same as gathering and making the wine at the correct time of year, but it is still preferable to going out and buying a bottle of chateaux-plonk with which to celebrate the turning year. It is also an exquisite excuse to talk to the shop owner about new wine yeasts or other aids to brewing that he has and to restock your cupboard for the year to come.

If you did not finish off the rum pot at Yule, then do so now. Each sip brings back memories of the wine made during the year and echoes of summers gone. What better reminder of summers yet to come and the promise of a full and flavoursome future (rowan wine would also be an excellent drink at this time of year. The rowan has long been acknowledged as a protective tree which wards against evil and darkness strengthening the life energy of those who eat or drink the berries, and bringing enlightenment and warmth. What could be more welcoming at this cold time of year?

Lyn Baylis

WINE RECIPES

All recipes make approximately one gallon of wine.

Dandelion Wine

Ingredients:

6 pints dandelion heads (take off as much green as possible - but do not press them down)
2 lemons
1 orange
1lb raisins
1 teaspoon tannin (or strong black tea)
3lb sugar
1 gallon water
Yeast and nutrient

Method:

Place dandelions in large pan, add rinds and boil for 10-15 minutes. Put sugar into bucket and pour liquid onto this, stir well and add fruit juice, pour over boiling water, cover with cloth or lid and leave for 2 days. Stir well every day, keeping the bucket covered.

On day three, pour into large pan, add sugar and rinds and boil for 10 -15 minutes. Return to the bucket, and add fruit juice and pulp (no pith). Allow to cool to blood temperature, then add wine yeast, nutrient and tea. Keep covered and leave for a further three days and keep the temperature warm to allow yeast to work.

On day six or seven, strain into the demijohn and fit fermentation locks. After several weeks, the wine will begin to clear and a sediment starts to form at the bottom of the jar. The wine is now ready to be siphoned into a second fermentation jar through a length of plastic tubing; this process is called "racking." Try not to let any of the sediment from the bottom of the jar get into the new jar. You can, if you wish, make up the small amount of wine left behind in the old jar, by adding cool boiled water to the new jar. Fit a new bung and fermentation lock (or sterilise the old ones before re-fitting) and leave for several more weeks.

The clearing process does take time, but patience is usually rewarded and it is rare for wine not to clear. Once the bubbling stops, you know the fermenting process is complete! At this time, you can either rack the wine again into a new jar and replace the bung and fermentation lock with a new bung/cork without the hole or, after sterilising a number of bottles, rack the wine into individual bottles, and cork them. (Corking machines are simple to use and relatively inexpensive.) Bottles should be stored on their sides so that the corks are covered with wine. Likewise, before opening a bottle of wine, let it first stand upright for a few hours to allow any sediment to settle to the bottom.

Keep all wines for at least 6 months. The longer you can leave it the better!

Nettle Wine

Ingredients:

4 pints nettle tops (should be young and tender)
2 lemons
½ oz root ginger
3- 3½ lb of Sugar
7 – 8 pts water
Yeast
Nutrient

Method:

Collect 4 pints of tender young nettle tops and rinse well. Place them into 2 pints of water. Add bruised ginger and lemon rinds and simmer for 45 minutes. Strain the mixture into a bucket and add the remaining water. Now add the sugar and lemon juice from both lemons. Stir until sugar completely dissolves. When the mixture is lukewarm (room temperature), add the yeast and yeast nutrient.

Cover the bucket with a clean cloth or lid, remembering to stir daily for 4-5 days. Siphon into a demijohn and add the airlock. Leave until the wine starts to clear, then rack into a clean jar. You may need to repeat this process again, then leave for approximately three months more before bottling.

Lyn Baylis

Birch Sap Wine

Ingredients:

1 gallon birch sap
2 lemons
1 sweet orange
½ pint of white wine concentrate
1 Seville orange
3 lbs Sugar
Yeast and nutrient

Method:

The sap must be collected when the sap is rising. Make sure that the tree you tap is established and around 1 foot in diameter. Bore into the tree sufficiently far to access the sap but no further. Fit a beer or wine barrel tap and insert tubing to allow passage of sap. A gallon of sap will take approximately three days to collect. Ensure that the hole is plugged up afterwards.

Peel the oranges and lemons and boil rinds in the sap for 20 minutes. Add sufficient water to restore the volume to one gallon then pour into a bucket containing sugar and concentrate, fruit juice and yeast. Cover well and leave in a warm place until the initial fermentation has slowed down. Strain and pour into demijohn and fit an airlock. Leave for three months and then siphon into second fermentation jar and leave until the fermentation finished.

Young Oak Leaf Wine

Ingredients:

1 gallon oak leaves (not pressed down)
Sugar to taste (3 lbs produces a medium-dry wine with an excellent flavour)
2 lemons or two teaspoons of citric acid
1 gallon water
Standard wine yeast and yeast nutrient

Method:

Pick the soft oak leaves and place in a large basin/bucket. Pour over 4 pints of boiling water, then cover the bucket with a clean cloth and leave for 12 hours. Put the sugar into a large saucepan with the remaining 4 pints of water and bring this to the boil, stirring until the sugar dissolves. Once the sugar is dissolved, take the pan off the heat and add the strained lemon juice before pouring into the bucket containing oak leaves. Stir well and allow mixture to steep until it is reduced to blood temperature.

Strain the oak leaf/water mixture into a fermentation jar, add the activated yeast and yeast nutrient and shake well. Now fit the rubber bung or cork into the neck of the jar and insert a glass or plastic fermentation lock which will fit firmly into the hole in the bung. Place the jar in a warm place, away from fluctuating temperatures. After several weeks, the wine will begin to clear and a sediment starts to form at the bottom of the jar. The wine is now ready to be siphoned into a second fermentation jar through a length of plastic tubing. Try not to let any of the sediment from the bottom of the jar get into the new jar. You can if you wish, make up the small amount of wine left behind in the old jar by adding cool boiled water to the new jar. Fit a new bung and fermentation lock (or sterilise the old ones before re-fitting) and leave for several more weeks.

Hawthorn Wine

Ingredients:

4 pints hawthorn blossom (don't squash down the blossom)
2 ½ - 3 lbs sugar
2 lemons
2 Oranges
1 gallon water
1 teaspoon of grape tannin or ¼ pint very strong tea
Yeast & nutrient

Method:

Boil all water if possible in one big pan. If you are unable to do so, then use sufficient water to dissolve the sugar. Add the lemon and orange rind (take care not to include the white pith) and the juice of one lemon. Leave this to simmer for half an hour. Pour into a plastic bucket (if necessary add the remainder of the boiling water to bring it up to 1 gallon). When this mixture has cooled to body temperature, add the yeast and yeast nutrient (with flower wines it is good practice to add a good yeast nutrient). Leave for 24 hours, then add freshly picked flowers.

Stir well and leave in a closed bucket for a further eight days, remembering to stir the mixture every day. At the end of this period, strain the mush through a sieve or muslin bag into a demijohn and fit an airlock. Rack for the first time when it clears, approximately three months later, and again a second time three months later. In six months, it should be ready to bottle and enjoy.

Gorse Wine

Ingredients:

1 gallon gorse flowers
2 oranges
2 lemons
3 lb sugar
1 teaspoon grape tannin or 1/4 pint very strong tea
1 gallon water
Yeast

Method:

Place gorse in water, bring to the boil and simmer for 15 - 20 minutes, remove the flowers, squeezing well to extract all the liquid. Add the sugar, lemon and orange juice and the skins, making sure there is no pith included. Allow the mixture to cool until it is lukewarm and then add the tannin, wine yeast and yeast nutrient. Stir well for three days, keeping the must well covered. After three days, strain into a fermenting jar and fit an airlock. Keep in a cool place and syphon off the must after three months and then again if necessary before bottling. It will be ready to drink in about six months.

Rose Petal Wine

To obtain a rose coloured wine, deep red varieties of rose should be used. The intensity of the perfume varies naturally with different types of rose. The older types usually have a richer perfume. White petals, or white and yellow petals will make a white wine. Rose petals can be collected daily, placed in a plastic bag and frozen until you have enough to make the wine

Ingredients:

- 4 pints of strongly scented rose petals
- 2.5 - 3 lbs sugar
- 1 orange
- 2 lemons
- 1 lb raisins
- 1 gallon water
- Yeast and nutrient

Method:

First wash and chop raisins then place water, sugar and thinly peeled rind of the orange and two lemons in a pan and bring to the boil. Once it is lukewarm, pour the liquid over the rose petals and add the juice from the fruit and chopped raisins. (make sure that there is no pith). Sir well and add the wine yeast and nutrient. Cover it with a clean cloth or lid and leave to ferment, stirring daily for seven days. After seven days strain off the liquid into a fermentation jar and leave to ferment out, racking if necessary. The clearing and fermentation process usually takes three - six months, but this wine is better left for a year.

Elderflower Wine

Ingredients:

1 pint flowers (approx. 5-8 heads)
2.5 - 3lb sugar
2 lemons
1 Orange
½ lb of raisins or ¼ pt grape concentrate
1 teaspoon grape tannin
Yeast and nutrient

Method:

Remove flowers from heads with a fork or trim with a pair of scissors. Boil water and pour onto flowers adding sugar, grape concentrate, lemon and orange juice. Let the mixture cool until it is lukewarm (room temperature) and then add grape tannin yeast and nutrient. Leave this covered in a warm place for five days, stirring each day. On the fifth day, strain into a fermenting jar and fit an airlock. Leave until the sediment sinks to the bottom and then rack the wine. You may well need to rack again approximately two months later before you bottle it. Leave for at least 6 months before drinking.

Lyn Baylis

Sparkling Elderflower Wine

(Elderflower Champagne)

Ingredients:

7 large heads of elderflowers
2 lemons
1.5 lbs of sugar
2 tablespoons of white wine vinegar
1 gallon of water

Method:

Boil the water and pour it over the sugar. Wait until this mixture is cold and then throw in the flower heads, sliced lemons and add the white wine vinegar. Let this mixture stand for twenty-four hours. Strain and bottle. Cork it well (if you can, use Champagne type bottles or tie down the corks well) and allow to stand where it will not be disturbed. Moving this can result in corks popping or bottles shattering.

Strawberry Wine

Ingredients:

1 gallon strawberries
1 gallon water
3½ lbs of sugar
½ lb raisins
yeast and nutrient

Method:

Place the strawberries and water into a pan and bring to the boil slowly. Simmer gently for 15- 20 minutes. Strain the liquid on the sugar and raisins and stir well. When the liquid is lukewarm, add the yeast. Leave for a further 2 days stirring well, or until the initial fermentation has died down and then syphon off into a demijohn fitted with an airlock for it to ferment out. Rack if necessary after three months and when fermentation is complete bottle, and leave before drinking for 6 months.

Lyn Baylis

Blackberry Wine

Ingredients:

6lb blackberries
4lbs sugar
1 lemon
1 gallon water
Yeast and nutrient

Method:

Pick berries, and wash well. Crush with a potato masher and put into a bucket along with thinly peeled lemon rind. Pour one gallon of boiling water over this stir well and allow to stand for three days stirring daily. Strain this mixture onto the sugar and again stir well. Add the juice of the lemon. Leave this covered for 24 hours in a warm place and then strain into the fermenting jar and insert an airlock.

Fermentation can be very strong at first so do not fill fermenting jar to the very top. Leave about a pint of the liquid separate and add after the initial fermentation surge. Top up with cold water and re-fit airlock. Leave to clear before racking, which is usually three months.

Plum Wine

Ingredients:

4lb plums
1 sliced lemon
¼ root ginger
3 lb sugar

Method:

Cut up the plums and remove the stones, Bruise the ginger and add to the plums, and sliced lemon. (You can add four cloves if you wish.)Pour the boiling water over the mixture and stir well. Cover and leave for three or four days stirring daily. Strain the liquid through muslin onto the sugar and warm the liquid until it is lukewarm. Add the yeast and leave in the bucket until the initial fermentation is over, which is usually two - three days. Pour into a demijohn and fit an airlock. Leave to ferment in a warm place.

Lyn Baylis

Morello Cherry Wine

Ingredients:

6 lbs cherries
4 lb sugar
1 tsp citric acid
1 gallon water
Yeast

Method:

This is a recipe where it is necessary to start the fermentation of the yeast before adding it to the ingredients. Stalk and wash cherries and place in brewing bucket, then pour on six pints of boiling water. Dissolve all the sugar in the remaining water and leave this to cool. Once the water is lukewarm, add citric acid and remove the cherry stones, best done by squeezing them out with your fingers, then cover and leave the mixture for three days, stirring every day.

On the fourth day, strain and gently squeeze the pulp. Mix in half the sugar syrup and the activated yeast and ferment in a tightly closely cover bucket for one week. Keep the remainder of the sugar syrup well covered. (The fridge is the best place.)

Seven days later, mix in half of the remaining syrup. Stir well, before pouring the remaining mixture into a demijohn and fitting an airlock. Allow the mixture to ferment out and then rack and bottle. Let this wine mature for at least a year.

Homemade Wine for Seasonal Festivals

Garden Cherry Wine

Ingredients:

4 lbs sweet cherries
2 lb cooking cherries (slightly sour)
3lbs sugar
1 gallon water
Wine yeast

Method:

Chop up the fruit in a large bowl and cover with water. Leave for three days, stirring daily. Strain onto the sugar and heat gently, stirring well to dissolve the sugar. When lukewarm, remove from heat and pour into a fermenting jar or demijohn and add the yeast. Insert an airlock and leave in a warm place for ferment. Taste after three weeks and if it's not sweet enough, add ¼ lb sugar and stir well. Leave for a couple of weeks until fermentation has finished and bottle.

Lyn Baylis

Mead - Honey Wine

Ingredients:

3 lb honey for a dry wine.
2 tablespoons strong cold tea (or 0.25 tsp of tannin)
6 pints water
juice of 1 lemon (sweet wine add juice of two lemons)
Chablis yeast and nutrient

Method:

Activate the yeast before you start the preparations.

Put warm (not boiling) water into a saucepan and add the honey, stir well until all the honey is dissolved.

Add the tannin and lemon juice.

Allow this mixture to heat to 66C and simmer for a few minutes. Take off any froth from the top, cover and leave to cool down again. When this is lukewarm add nutrient and stir well before adding the activated yeast. Cover tightly and leave in a warm place for two - three days.

Transfer to a demijohn and fit a bung/cork and an airlock and place in a dark and warm (but not too warm) place to ferment. Once the fermentation has settled down top up to the shoulder with cooled boiled water to within an inch of the cork. Place in a cool place until fermentation is complete and there are no bubbles in the airlock. This will take 4 - 6 weeks.

As the mead clears, it will be necessary to siphon off the lees into another demijohn at least once before bottling. On the last racking when the mead is clear add a Campden tablet and top the demijohn up with water again. It usually takes a year from start to finish but is much better is left for longer. The best mead is 2 years old at least! Do try to leave it that long it will be worth it.

For a sweet mead:

(If you want to make sweet mead it will be an investment for you to purchase a hydrometer and use it to test the SG Specific Gravity as your mead ferments.)

Start the mead off in the same way as directed but use the juice of two lemons. Once the initial fermentation slows down or when Specific Gravity has dropped to less than 1.005 add a further 4oz of sugar. A few weeks later do the same again or check the SG (Specific Gravity) if it is less than 1.005 add a further 4 oz.

Continue this process each time adding 4 oz sugar. This is called feeding the yeast When the fermentation is finished stir in enough honey to achieve the correct sweetness for you. You may find you have added a further 2 lbs of honey to the brew, and the result will be a strong mead with 16 or 17% alcohol. Leave the mead for another couple of weeks and make sure the fermentation has stopped before bottling. Leave as long as you can a year is the minimum time for storage, 2 or 3 years produces an even better mead.

Lyn Baylis

Apple Wine

Ingredients:

6lb apples
3lb sugar
½ lb chopped raisins
1 lemon
1 gallon water
Yeast

Method:

Cut the apple into small pieces. Don't worry about skin or brown patches. Windfalls are entirely acceptable. Boil for approximately fifteen minutes in as much of the water as is possible. Strain liquid onto the sugar and the thinly peeled lemon rind. Stir well and add remaining boiled water to make up to one gallon. When liquid is lukewarm, add the yeast. Cover and leave in a warm place in the sealed container for a week, stirring each day.

After seven days, strain and press the mush through a muslin bag into a demijohn and then pour into fermenting jar. Insert an airlock and leave for a further four weeks. Syphon the wine into another clean, dry demijohn and add the chopped raisins. Leave a further six months to mature, then syphon into clean bottles for storing.

This wine will be ready to drink in approximately six months, but, like most wines, it will be at its best nearer to a year, just right for the Lammas festival. If you want to be a purist, you can skip the raisins, but you would then require twenty-four lbs of apples.

Elderberry Wine

Ingredients:

- 4-5 lbs elderberries
- 1 gallon water
- 2 tablespoons ground ginger or ½ oz root ginger (optional)
- 3½ lbs sugar
- 1 lemon
- Yeast

Method:

Pick the elderberries on a dry day. The best way to separate them from the stalks is to use the prongs of a fork. Place the berries into a plastic bucket and squash them to release the juice. Bring the water to the boil, and pour this onto the mush. Cover the container with a clean cloth or lid and leave for three days stirring daily.

After three days, strain the liquid through a muslin bag onto the lemon peel and ginger (bruise the ginger root well), bring the mixture to the boil and simmer for 10 minutes, then pour in the sugar and stir thoroughly to ensure all the sugar dissolves. Leave the mixture until it is lukewarm. Stir in the yeast. (With most fruit wines it is best to activate the yeast before you add it.) Finally, pour into the demijohn and leave to clear.

Lyn Baylis

Rosehip Wine

Ingredients:

2lb rose hips
3lb sugar
7 pts water
1 teaspoon citric acid
1 tsp Pectic enzyme
Yeast and nutrient

Method:

Wash well and cut in half before crushing and then add the sugar. Pour on boiling water and stir well to dissolve all the sugar, Allow to cool to room temperature, before adding pectin, acid yeast and nutrient. Cover closely and leave in warm place for two weeks, stirring daily. Strain into fermenting jar and fit airlock, after 3 months rack into clean demijohn and then leave for a further three months. Then rack a final time when the wine is clear bottle and leave for 6 months at least.

Sloe Wine

Ingredients:

3lb sloes (best picked after the first frost)
0.50 of raisins
3lb sugar
7 pts water
Pectic enzyme
Yeast and nutrient

Method:

Pour boiling water over the sloes and mash well. Add raisins and 2lb of the sugar and stir well. When cooled to room temp, add pectic enzyme and a day later, stir in yeast and nutrient. Cover well and leave in a warm place for at least a week stirring daily.

Once the initial fermentation has calmed down strain and pour in the remaining sugar into fermenting jar and fit airlock. Leave to ferment for a month in warm place. If the wine tastes bitter, a little more sugar can be added at this stage. Rack and allow fermentation to continue in a cooler place.

Bottle when the wine has cleared. Leave for a year before drinking.

Lyn Baylis

Sloe Gin

Ingredients:

12 oz sloes
6 oz caster sugar
1 standard bottle of gin

Method:

Use plump dark sloes. Wash, stalk and prick them all over. (Placing them in the freezer can cause them to split, thus saving the time-consuming job of pricking all over.) Place the sloes in a jar or other container in layers, covering each layer with sugar. Pour over the gin and leave for three months shaking occasionally to mix up.

After three months, strain the liquid and discard the sloes. Bottle the mixture and ensure it is well sealed. Store for at least one year to mature.

The discarded sloes can be used in all sorts of wonderful desserts!

Homemade Wine for Seasonal Festivals

Rowan Berry Wine

Ingredients:

3lbs berries
3lbs sugar
½ pint of grape concentrate
2 lemons
7 pts water
Yeast and nutrient

Method:

Take off berries from a branch with a fork, or cut close with a pair of scissors. Add rind of lemons. Pour on boiling water and leave for three to four days. Strain onto the sugar and add concentrate and lemon juice. Stir well to dissolve sugar. Allow to cool at room temp and then add yeast and nutrient. Cover well and leave in a warm place for two weeks stirring every day. At the end of this period, strain into fermentation jar and add airlock. Rack the mixture when clear and then bottle a few months later.

Lyn Baylis

Mixed Berry Wine - English Port

Ingredients:

2lb elderberries
2lb blackberries
2lb sloes
2 lbs blackcurrants
1/4 pt (one can) red grape concentrate
3 lbs sugar
1 gallon water
Vitamin B tablet
Port yeast and nutrient

Method:

The amounts of fruit can be varied, but I think this recipe produces the best combination wine. During the year, I invariably end up with extra fruit. Freezers are fantastic for saving this fruit until the winter when it all gets added together to produce a lovely rich red wine.

Place the fruit into a buck and crush well. Cover the sugar with some of the water and bring to the boil, then pour it over the crushed fruit. When the mixture is lukewarm, stir in the grape concentrate and pectolase. The following day, add the vitamin B, yeast, nutrient and remaining water. Ferment in the bucket for at least five days and then strain into a demi-jar and make up to one gallon. Allow to ferment out before racking and bottling in the usual way.

WASSAIL BOWL

Ingredients:

3 small cooking apples
3 oz brown sugar
½ bottle of cider
12 cloves
1 tsp powdered ginger
Grated nutmeg to taste
1 bottle apple wine

Method:

Wash and core the apples and fill them with the brown sugar and a little cider. Push four cloves into each apple until they no longer protrude, then bake the apples until they are soft enough to mash. Remove the apple skins and discard along with the cloves. Sprinkle on the powdered ginger and the rest of the sugar and some grated nutmeg. Mash all the ingredients together, slowly adding the rest of the cider. Stir in the apple wine before pouring the liquor into a saucepan and heating slowly to 60°c. Keep stirring gently.

Ladle into individual glasses or place in a bowl and allow guest to help themselves.

Lyn Baylis

Wheat Whiskey

Ingredients:

1 pt wheat
2 lbs sultanas (chopped)
2 large potatoes
2 lbs demerara sugar
2 lemons - juice and grated rind
½ cup of cold strong tea
1 tsp pectic enzyme - from brewing shop
1 tsp yeast nutrient
All-purpose yeast

Method:

Place the wheat, sultanas, sugar, and pectic enzyme into a bucket. Add the peeled and grated potatoes to this mixture. Pour on six pints of tepid water and mix well. Cover and leave in a warm place for twenty-four hours then stir in the yeast and yeast nutrient. Cover the bucket once more and leave the mixture to stand for a further ten - fourteen days, stirring every day.

Strain off the must into a demijohn and fit bung and an airlock. Keep warm and when the wine starts to clear, rack and add a crushed Campden tablet.

Rack again when a sediment forms and the wine is quite clear. Leave for at least three months before bottling.

Dried Fruit Wines

Follow the recipe as for fresh fruit, allowing the fruit to hydrate first, by soaking overnight in water, or pure fruit juice. If you use fruit juice, decrease the amount of water required by the recipe.

Frozen Fruit Wines

Allow the fruit to defrost and then weigh it. Follow the recipe for fresh fruit, ensuring that you have sufficient fruit as required.

Lyn Baylis

Tinned Fruit Wines

It is possible to mark some superb light wine from tinned fruit. You will need to take into account the liquid into which the fruit has been placed. If it is sugar-free or in a natural juice (e.g. apple juice), then reduce the amount of water required to ferment the fruit by an equal amount.

If it is in a light sugar syrup, that that will ferment readily. Watch out for cans that contain preservatives, as these will impede the fermentation process.

The exact quantity in each can is not significant, providing the total amount of fruit used comes to around 3lbs / 1.35kg. To obtain the best results, a mixture of fruits usually produces the best wine.

Ingredients:

- 3lb of mixed fruit, e.g. blackberries, black cherries, blackcurrants and damsons
- 1 small 200g can grape concentrate
- 1tsp grape tannin
- Pectic enzyme
- 2tsp tartaric acid
- 1 Campden tablet
- 800g sugar
- A good wine yeast, e.g. a port wine or Bordeaux wine yeast
- Yeast nutrient

Method:

Drain off and save the syrup, preferably in a fridge. Remove the fruit stones and crush the fruit. Place the crushed fruit into a bucket with 4 pints of water, the pectic enzyme, 1 crushed Campden tablet, and 1tsp tartaric acid. Cover and leave this mixture for a good twenty-four hours. Add the concentrated grape juice, tannin, activated yeast and nutrient and leave it to ferment in the bucket for a further four days, stirring each day.

Boil the sugar, the remaining acid and 1 pint of water for 20 minutes, and then leave the mixture to cool.

Remove the fruit by filtering through muslin or similar, gently squeezing to get maximum juice. Next mix in the fruit syrup, the sugar syrup and pour the must into a demijohn. Top this up to the gallon mark if necessary and fit an airlock. Leave to ferment out at room temperature.

When the mixture stops bubbling, decant it into a storage jar and top up again if necessary with boiled water. Leave for a further eight weeks and then decant again if there is still sediment in the demijohn. Store until the wine is clear and then bottle. Keep for nine months before drinking.

Final Thoughts

I trust that you have had a good brewing year and that you experienced firsthand many of the properties and gifts of the individual wine. So use your judgement. What is it you most need at this time of year? Think about this and then go and select one of the wines you made earlier.

There is no better feeling, having decided what you most need in life than to start proceedings by opening your own bottle of homemade wine.

Enjoy!

Basic Requirements for Country Wines

Sterilising solution/tablets

Cleanliness is the primary consideration with homemade wines. It is essential to ensure that all the equipment is kept sterile or sterilised before use, but sterilising solutions are readily available in powder or tablet form and, providing the instructions are followed, your wine will remain clear of any bacterial infection. In the absence of sterilising solutions, "Campden tablets" are always a handy and a good standby or if you have a young family, the sterilizing solutions for babies' bottles work just as well with winemaking equipment.

A new white plastic bucket

It should have a tightly fitted lid and a capacity of 2.5 gallons (9 litres) minimum. It is best if it is white because coloured buckets have been dyed and can contaminate the wine; plastic because it is the easier to keep clean.

Plastic spoon

Plastic minimizes the chance of bacterial infection. Wooden spoons, unfortunately, do soften and crack with age and use and are more inclined to harbour bacteria. Metal spoons can set off a chemical reaction when in contact with yeast or acids.

Straining bag.

There are readily obtainable nylon bags, but an ordinary piece of cheesecloth or muslin can be utilized or even an old stocking, provided it has been boiled to remove the dye.

Plastic funnel

To help when straining liquid from the bucket into the jar.

Plastic tubing

to decant the wine, from one jar to another or when bottling finished wine.

Demijohn

(or fermentation jar which holds 1 gallon of wine) with rubber or cork bung.(A second demijohn will be needed approximately two months later.) I managed to pick up all my demijohns from car boot sales, it is worth looking out for secondhand.

An air/fermentation lock

To allow the gases to escape from the wine while keeping out unwanted oxygen and to prevent fruit flies and other unwanted additives from gaining access to your wine.

Corks and Corking machine

Corks are relatively inexpensive and can be purchased from any good brewing shop or online. The corking machine does not have to be complicated or expensive, but makes corking your bottles easier and reduces the risk of the corks getting loose and allowing oxygen or fruit flies into the wine.

A large saucepan

Usually, a jam making saucepan is ideal. Remember, you have to be able to boil your contents and lift full the saucepan from the hob. I have just started to use a small urn when I need to boil water to pour onto the ingredients so that I don't need to lift the heavy saucepan.

Wine yeast

It is the yeast that turns the sugar into alcohol. These days there are high-quality wine yeasts sealed in aluminium foil packs which can be added to your wine once the mixture is lukewarm. This takes the worry away for beginners and will make an excellent wine. If you are using baker's yeast, then place 1 level teaspoon of yeast per gallon of wine into a cup half to three-quarters full of lukewarm water. Cover this mixture with cling film or a clean tea cloth and leave in a warm place for approximately 20 minutes before adding it to the must.

Wine Nutrient

Many country wines have insufficient nutrients in the ingredients, therefore, to achieve the best wines you may need to add a yeast nutrient.

It is possible now to buy wine yeast with nutrient already added which is ideal for newcomers first starting out. It is probably the best type of yeast you can get and as you get more proficient you can start buying the more specialized wine yeasts and nutrients.

Sugar to Taste

2.5 - 3 lbs of sugar for each gallon of water produces a medium-dry wine with an excellent flavour.

Ingredients as per Recipe

If quantity is given as pints, quarts, etc., it requires you to fill the measure to that level with flowers or leaves, but not pressing down the ingredient

Note Book

Keep a note of the ingredients you use, and the results. next time you make the wine you can vary the sugar to taste, or add other ingredients.

OTHER USEFUL INGREDIENTS FOR YOUR STOCK CUPBOARD:

Campden tablets to sterilize equipment and stop fermentation.

Citric acid (instead of lemon juice) is used when there is insufficient acid in the ingredients to promote a good fermentation.

Pectic enzyme to help extract the flavour from the fruit and assist in producing a clear wine. (It must be added to the mix at room temperature a full 24 hours before you add the yeast.)

A small tin of grape concentrate for when a wine needs a little more body.

Glossary of Terms Used

Fermentation: The action of the yeast upon the ingredients.

Must: The mixture of ingredients to which you will add the yeast.

Lees: The sediment that will settle to the bottom of the demijohn during fermentation.

Demijohn: A one gallon container used for brewing wine.

Airlock: A glass or plastic air trap which allows carbon dioxide to escape the wine but prevents oxygen from entering it. This will force the yeast to obtain oxygen from the sugar, and the more sugar that is broken down, the more alcohol is produced.

Racking: Straining the wine off the lees once the sediment has settled. It is a good idea to rack wine at three months of age and again at six months of age. This process will help produce a clear wine.

Syphoning: A way of racking that uses a piece of plastic or rubber tubing.

Sediment: The mixture left in the bottom of the bucket or container when the liquid is strained off into a fermentation jar.

Tannin: A bitter substance found in grape stalks, pips and skins that give character to a wine.

Problem Page

You hopefully shouldn't have to worry about this page.

I have made a note of some of the problem areas which can occur but, to be honest, they don't happen that often. As long as you pay attention to your wine and stir the must every day, once or twice if possible, it is unlikely that you will need to pay attention to this section.

Over-sweet wine

If you are going to have a problem, this will probably be it! Stick to the recipe and don't use too much sugar initially. (More sugar doesn't mean more alcohol.)

If it does happen, the easiest thing is to blend it with one where you have used similar ingredients which you think may be a little on the dry side or with a dry rhubarb wine.

Wine which is too dry

Depending on whether you are going to drink the wine shortly (1) or store it (2), this problem is very easy to rectify:

(1) Pour the wine into a jug or container and add sugar to taste.

(2) Make up a sugar syrup solution and add sulphite (instructions for use on the tub). Alternatively you can sweeten with glycerin or any of the sugar substitutes, including artificial sweeteners, but do not add too much, as these will not ferment, and will leave you with an over sweet wine.

Taints and Smells (that are not too strong)

Usually caused by a bacterial action in tainted plastic containers (buckets) or demijohns and bottles that have not been sterilised properly.

Take out approximately 1 pint of wine and slowly add charcoal to it. Make a careful note of how much you have used and when the taint or smell is gone, add in the same proportions to the rest of the wine.

Failure to Clear

This can be brought about by over-boiling the ingredients or from straining the wine too soon, or not sufficiently careful in the racking procedure. Often if you move the wine and place it somewhere cold, it will clear in its own good time. However, if you are in too much of a hurry for this you can try filtering the wine through filter paper, or using wine finings (your brewery shop will advise which is best to use)

Acetification - or wine that has turned to vinegar

This will only occur where the wine has been stored badly and oxygen has got into the brew. If you notice this early on when the smell is not strong, it can probably be stopped by adding a Campden tablet to the wine. Leave this for 24 hours and then add a new yeast. You will need to start the yeast off before adding it to the wine and ensure that it is working vigorously. If the taste and smell are both strong, then I'm afraid the only solution is to pour the wine away. This breaks every winemaker's heart, but thankfully doesn't happen often.

Mousey smelling and tasting wine

The smell is a microbiological fault caused by the spoilage yeasts belonging to the genera Brettanomyces and Dekkera and by the lactic acid bacteria, Lactobacillus hilgardii and Lactobacillus brevis. It is found in wine after the fermentation is finished and the wine has been stored. It is very difficult to get rid of; you can try charcoal as above, but you have to use so much of it, the colour and the flavour have usually gone by the time you get rid of the smell. Unfortunately, if the mousey smell is bad, it is probably best just to pour the wine away.

***

As I stated earlier, if you are careful, you should be able to produce a good wine, and will not need this page.

I will, however, tell you about the cherry wine I made using tinned cherries. Somehow, after putting all the ingredients into a bucket and covering it with a cloth, I managed to forget about it. To this day, I don't know how, but with all the preparations for Yule, it was pushed behind pots and pans in the larder and sat there out of sight for months. When I eventually found the bucket the must had a thick and hard layer on it which had the appearance of a massive meringue. I pushed gently on one side of this hard lump it shifted vertically so that I got a wet finger. Tentatively, I tasted the wine. It was fantastic, sweet, rich and fruity. I was however I little worried about the meringue on top. Would it have affected the wine? Was it still ok to drink? In my usual fashion, I went down the road to Ernie Turner, the local wine expert and persuaded him to come and have a look. He took one look and laughed loudly. 'My goodness,' he said (or words to that effect). 'What you've got there, girl, is nature's own barrier that this wine has set up to keep the oxygen out.' And so saying, he removed the meringue. Asking me for a glass, he sampled the brew. Like me, he was stunned that it tasted so good, and, much to my pleasure, asked if he could have a bottle of it. Bless him, knowing I would have to bottle it immediately nature's own fermentation lock was removed, he stayed and helped me strain the wine and bottle it before he went home.

I include this not to encourage you to leave or forget about your wine! But rather to remind you that sometimes nature steps in and does her own thing, and there is very little we can do when that happens. Sometimes it is a ruined wine and all you can do is tip it away and put it down to experience, but sometimes the resulting brew can be very, very good.

Imperial to Metric

1 ounce = 28.35 grams

1 lbs (pound) = 453.59 grams

1 gallon = 4.55 litres

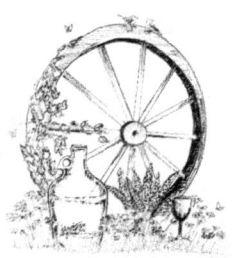

Index

A

agricultural calendar 22
alcohol 11, 13, 18, 30, 31, 94, 110, 113, 114
angels 25
Anthesteria, festival of 15
Aphrodite 50, 55
apple 54, 60, 95, 102
apple wine 52, 53, 102
April 32, 35
August 4, 24, 52
Autumn Equinox 59, 60

B

Bacchanalia 16
Bacchus 15
beer 13, 15, 52, 60, 81
bees 35
Bel 39
Belenus 39
Beltane . 23, 34, 36, 38, 39, 40, 47, 65
Beowulf 56
Bible 16
birch 81
blackberries 24, 60, 61, 62, 63, 89, 101, 105

blackcurrants 71, 101, 105
blackthorn 68
Bride 74
Bridie 74
Britain 16, 52

C

Campden tablet 93, 103, 105, 116
Candlemas 23, 33, 57, 73, 74
carbon dioxide 18, 113
Carthaginians 16
Catholic Church 16
Cerne Abbas 49
chalice 16
champagne 49
cherry 55, 91, 92, 105, 116
Christian Communion 16
Christmas 23, 69, 70, 71
cloves 90, 102
Cornwall 70
Cowslip 42
Crème de Cassis 71

D

damsons 54, 61, 105
dandelion 33, 35, 78

119

Darwen 41
December 23, 70
Devon 70
dog rose 50, 55, 63
Dryads 25, 26

E

Egypt 13, 72
Elder 49, 61
elderberry 61, 96, 101
Elderflower 49, 86
Elderflower Champagne *See* Sparkling Elderflower Wine
element of air 35
element of earth 55
element of fire 36, 45, 67
element of water 55
equinox 23, 32, 33, 34, 36, 58, 59, 60, 61
ethyl alcohol 18

F

February 15, 74
fermentation 9, 13, 14, 15, 18, 78, 79, 81, 82, 85, 88, 89, 90, 91, 92, 93, 94, 98, 100, 105, 109, 110, 112, 113, 116, 117
fertility rituals 16
Findhorn 25
flowers .. 9, 10, 14, 19, 23, 25, 26, 27, 28, 29, 35, 42, 43, 45, 54, 55, 60, 62, 73, 74, 75, 83, 84, 86, 87, 111
Frey 72
Freya 42, 50
fruit . 9, 10, 18, 19, 21, 23, 24, 26, 50, 54, 55, 57, 58, 60, 63, 66, 71, 76, 78, 81, 85, 92, 96, 101, 104, 105, 106, 110, 112

G

Gaul 16
gin 57, 99
ginger 60, 80, 90, 96, 102
Goddess 14
gorse 44, 45, 84
grain 18, 19, 53
grape concentrate .86, 100, 101, 105, 112

H

Halloween 23, 64, 65
Hallowmas 23
Harvest Moon 59
hawthorn 40, 41, 60, 83
Hereford 74
Hippocrates 36
holly 59, 61, 71
honey 56, 93, 94
hooded ones 25
Horus 14

I

Imbolc 23, 33, 34, 67, 73, 74, 75
Inundation ceremony 13
Ishtar 14

J

January 23
July 24
June 23

L

Lady Day 23
Lammas 23, 51, 52, 53, 59, 95
Last Supper 16
leaf 18, 25, 28, 36, 41, 82
lemon... 80, 82, 83, 84, 86, 89, 90, 93, 95, 96, 100, 112
Liber 15

Lindisfarne 56
loaf mass 52
Lugh 52
Lughnasadh 23, 52

M

March 23, 32, 35, 36, 41
May . 6, 23, 24, 36, 38, 39, 40, 41, 42, 43, 54
may blossom 40
May Day 23, 38, 39, 40, 43
mead 56, 71, 93, 94
Mercurial 35
Mesopotamia 14
Michaelmas 23
Midsummer 23, 47, 48
Midsummer Day 23, 47, 48
Moon 15, 48, 52
Morello Cherry 91
mulled wine 75
must 9, 84, 103, 106, 110

N

Nettle 36, 80
Nile 13
Norse Goddess 42, 50
November 65
nutmeg 102

O

Oak 33, 34, 36, 41, 43, 68, 82
oak leaf 36, 41
oak leaf wine 36, 41
Osiris 14

P

Pagat 14
pastoral calendar 22
pectic enzyme 103
Pectic enzyme .. 97, 98, 103, 105, 112

plum 54, 55, 90
poisonous ingredients 19
potato wine 18

R

raisins 29, 78, 85, 88, 95, 98
religious ceremonies 13, 16
Renen-utet 14
Roman Empire 15
Roman Senate 15
rose 40, 47, 48, 50, 63, 85, 97
rose petals 50, 85
rosehip 63, 97
rowan 61, 67, 76
rum pot 57, 76

S

Samhain 23, 64, 65
Scorpio 36
seasonal festivals 22
September 23, 59, 60
Shakespeare 35
silver birch 44
sloes 61, 68, 71, 98, 99, 101
Solstice 23
Sparkling Elderflower Wine .. 7, 49, 87
Spring Equinox 36
St Bridget 74
St George 33, 35
strawberries 24, 49, 50, 88
sugar 9, 18, 57, 78, 80, 81, 82, 83, 84, 85, 86, 87, 88, 89, 90, 91, 92, 94, 95, 96, 97, 98, 99, 100, 101, 102, 103, 105, 106, 110, 111, 113, 114, 115
sultanas 103
Sumerian 13, 14
Summer Solstice 23, 46, 47, 63
Sun. 27, 36, 39, 40, 45, 46, 47, 48, 49, 52, 53, 58, 66, 67, 68, 70, 71, 74,

75

T

Taliesin 56
tannin 78, 83, 84, 86, 93, 105, 106, 113
tartaric acid 105
tea 33, 43, 60, 78, 83, 84, 93, 103, 110

V

vegetable 9, 10, 18, 59, 60, 76
Venus 42, 44, 50, 55, 63
Vernal Equinox 23
vinegar 87, 115
Virgin Mary 74

W

Wheat 72, 103
wild rose 50
Winter Solstice 23, 69, 70, 71

Y

yeast 9, 13, 18, 78, 80, 81, 82, 83, 84, 85, 86, 88, 90, 91, 92, 93, 94, 95, 96, 97, 98, 100, 101, 103, 105, 106, 109, 110, 111, 112, 113, 116
Yule 23, 57, 69, 70, 71, 76, 116

PUBLISHED BY AVALONIA
www.avaloniabooks.co.uk